SPORT STRETCH

Michael J. Alter, MS

Leisure Press

Library of Congress Cataloging-in-Publication Data

Alter, Michael J., 1952-
  Sport stretch / by Michael J. Alter.
    p. cm.
  Includes bibliographical references.
  ISBN 0-88011-381-2
  1. Physical education and training. 2. Stretching exercises.
  I. Title.
  GV711.5.A45 1990
  613.7'1--dc20   89-27880
                                                   CIP

ISBN: 0-88011-381-2

Copyright © 1990 by Michael J. Alter

Developmental Editor: Holly Gilly; **Copyeditor:** Wendy Nelson; **Assistant Editors:** Valerie Hall and Timothy Ryan; **Proofreader:** Dianna Matlosz; **Production Director:** Ernie Noa; **Typesetters:** Cindy Pritchard and Brad Colson; **Text Design:** Keith Blomberg; **Text Layout:** Tara Welsch; **Cover Design:** Jack Davis; **Cover Photo:** Wilmer Zehr; **Illustrations:** Michael Richardson; **Model:** Linda Bosch; **Printer:** United Graphics

Printed in the United States of America   10 9 8 7

Leisure Press
A Division of Human Kinetics
Box 5076, Champaign, IL 61825-5076
1-800-747-4457

Canada: Human Kinetics, Box 24040, Windsor, ON N8Y 4Y9
1-800-465-7301 (in Canada only)

Europe: Human Kinetics, P.O. Box IW14, Leeds LS16 6TR, England
0532-781708

Australia: Human Kinetics, P.O. Box 80, Kingswood 5062, South Australia
618-374-0433

New Zealand: Human Kinetics, P.O. Box 105-231, Auckland 1
(09) 309-2259

To Aimee Michelle,
Josh,
and Emily

CONTENTS

PREFACE

During any given sports season, the sports sections of most newspapers print the names of players who are currently disabled. Look, for example, at a few of the names that were on such a list during a recent baseball season[1]:

- Mickey Hatcher, Los Angeles Dodgers— Pulled hamstring
- Rick Reuschel, San Francisco Giants— Groin pull
- Marvin Freeman, Philadelphia Phillies— Strained triceps
- Dave Meads, Houston Astros—Strained ligaments
- Danny Cox, St. Louis Cardinals—Torn ligaments

These represent just a few men from one league in one sport on one day whose injuries might have been prevented by a regular routine of stretching. There are many other athletes in many other sports who have been disabled by muscle and joint injuries—some during crucial times in the sport's season. Note the injuries of athletes like Magic Johnson of the Los Angeles Lakers, whose team lost the 1989 NBA championship after he was disabled by a pulled hamstring; or Mary Decker Slaney, who fared poorly in the 1500- and 3000-meter runs in the 1988 Olympics because of a pulled calf muscle. Probably the world's most infamous pulled hamstring was the one that injured 100-meter sprinter Ben Johnson. Because he knew the injury could ruin his chances of winning a medal in the Olympics in Seoul, he turned to steroids. Ultimately he was stripped of his world record time and his gold medal, and he lost numerous potential endorsements.[2] Clearly, such injuries can be devastating, but they can be minimized when athletes are fully stretched and have developed their optimum flexibility.

The purpose of this book is to help athletes and coaches reduce the risk of injury and improve sports performance by presenting basic knowledge that will provide

- an understanding of the factors related to flexibility and stretching, and
- a guide to over 300 stretching exercises designed primarily for the healthy athlete.

Part I introduces the basic principles of flexibility and stretching. Part II contains 29 sport-specific stretching routines. From these routines 12 stretches are illustrated that are of most benefit to participants in the related sports or events. Part III presents 311 stretches arranged in a systematic order by the muscle group or joints to be stretched and by their degree of difficulty or risk (which, of course, varies from athlete to athlete). Readers who are interested in doing further research on stretching and flexibility are encouraged to look through the appendix and the reference list at the end of the book.

In his famous maxims, Benjamin Franklin advises the reader to act with circumspection and care, in even the smallest matters.

> For want of a Nail the Shoe was lost; for want of a Shoe the Horse was lost; and for want of a Horse the Rider was lost, being overtaken and slain by the Enemy, all for want of Care about a Horse Shoe Nail.

As an athlete, you should also act with circumspection and care in even the smallest details of your sport. Whether you participate in sports for recreation or for competition, beginning and maintaining a regular stretching program could keep you from experiencing a disabling injury that would limit your enjoyment or success. The stretches in this book are a good way to start your injury prevention program and enhance your performance.

---

[1] From National League Disabled List. (1989, August 16). *USA Today*, p. 10C.

[2] From Conrad, R. (1988, November). Samolenko Outkicks Ivan. *Track & Field News*, p. 58; and Johnson, W.O. & Moore, K. (1988, October 3). The Loser. *Sports Illustrated*, pp. 20-27.

ACKNOWLEDGMENTS

I wish to express my gratitude to the many who made this work possible. My thanks go to the American Physical Therapy Association; the Benjamin/Cummings Publishing Company; Don W. Fawcett; Little, Brown and Company; and VCH Publishers, all of whom generously gave permission to reproduce their illustrative material.

I am once again indebted to the excellent work of artist Michael Richardson. Quoting a prior reviewer: "[It is] remarkable in that from such a simple presentation so much about the complex motions of the body can be expressed." These drawings indeed reflect the highest degree of craftsmanship.

I am also grateful to Leisure Press, a division of Human Kinetics Publishers, which made this project possible. Lastly, I wish to acknowledge Mr. Brian Holding, the director of Leisure Press; Ms. Holly Gilly, my developmental editor; and all other members of the Human Kinetics staff for their assistance throughout the production of this book.

Michael J. Alter

HOW
STRETCHING
WORKS

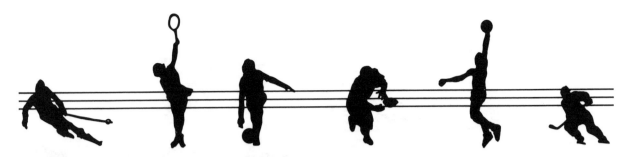

PART I

THE BENEFITS OF STRETCHING

Flexibility is the ability to move muscles and joints through their full ranges of motion. Flexibility is developed by stretching. However, stretching is good only when you stretch properly. Some of the many reasons why athletes should want to improve their flexibility through stretching exercises are shown in the shaded box.

Benefits of Stretching

- Stretching can enhance an athlete's physical fitness.
- Stretching can optimize an athlete's learning, practice, and performance of many types of skilled movements.
- Stretching can increase an athlete's mental and physical relaxation.
- Stretching can promote an athlete's development of body awareness.
- Stretching can reduce an athlete's risk of joint sprain or muscle strain.
- Stretching can reduce an athlete's risk of back problems.
- Stretching can reduce an athlete's muscular soreness.
- Stretching can reduce the severity of painful menstruation (dysmenorrhea) for female athletes.
- Stretching can reduce an athlete's muscular tension.

HOW MUSCLES ARE STRUCTURED

Two of the many intricate parts that make up the human body are the skeletal and the muscular systems. These systems are important because they provide the body with protection, support, and movement. Without structural support, your body would collapse under its own weight and be little more than a jellylike mass.

Your bones are the specialized support system of your body's skeleton, and to perform their support function they must be held together. Joints are points at which two or more bones connect, and the connections are performed primarily by ligaments, assisted by muscles.

The primary function of muscle tissue is to produce movement through its ability to contract and develop tension. Muscles are attached to bone by tendons. The place where a muscle attaches to a relatively stationary point on a bone is called the *origin*, and the end of the muscle that moves with the bone is known as the *insertion*. When the muscle contracts, it develops tension that is transmitted to the bones by the tendons, and movement takes place. Thus, movement is caused by the interaction of the muscular and the skeletal systems.

Although the function of the muscles is to produce movement by contracting and generating tension, the muscles must be relaxed during stretching. Let's look at the structure of a muscle to better understand this. Muscles come in various shapes and sizes and are comprised of progressively smaller units (see Figure 1). The *myofibrils* are the elements of your muscles that contract (shorten), relax, and elongate (stretch). These are composed of *sarcomeres*, which are represented in Figure 1 as repeating light and dark patterns. The sarcomeres are the functional units of the myofibrils, and they are primarily composed of thick *(myosin)* and thin *(actin)* interlocking myofilaments.

At present, muscles are hypothesized to function in the way described by *Huxley's sliding myofilament theory.* Basically, the muscle fibers receive a nerve impulse that causes the release of calcium ions stored in the muscle. In the presence of ATP (adenosine triphosphate), which is the "fuel" of the muscles, the calcium ions bind with the actin and myosin myofilaments to form an *electrostatic bond*. This bond can be likened to two opposing magnets attracting each other. As a result of this bond, the muscle

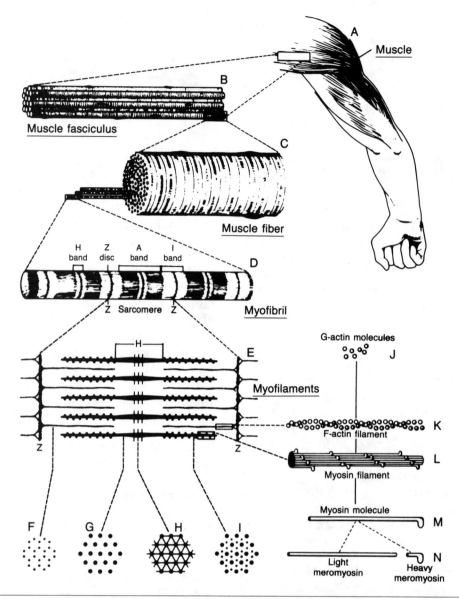

Figure 1. Organization of skeletal muscle tissue from the gross to the molecular level. F,G,H, and I are cross sections at the levels indicated. *Note.* From *A Textbook of Histology* (11th ed., p. 282) by D. Fawcett, 1986, Philadelphia: W.B. Saunders Company. Copyright 1986 by Don W. Fawcett. Reprinted by permission.

fibers shorten and develop tension. When the muscle fiber ceases to receive nerve impulses, it relaxes. The recoil of the elastic elements restores the myofilaments to their former uncontracted lengths.

In contrast, when the muscles are stretched the myofilaments reverse the interlinking effect that takes place during contraction. Research has shown that a sarcomere can be stretched to 150 percent of its resting-state length (see Figure 2). This has a major implication for all athletes: If the muscle is relaxed (and there is the absence

of any structural limitation) and if the connective tissues are properly stretched, *you* can achieve a split!

HOW MUSCLES RESPOND

Skeletal (or *voluntary*) muscles possess two distinct types of nerve-fiber receptors. These are the *muscle spindles* and the *Golgi tendon organs* (see Figure 3). Muscle spindles are encapsulated structures that run parallel

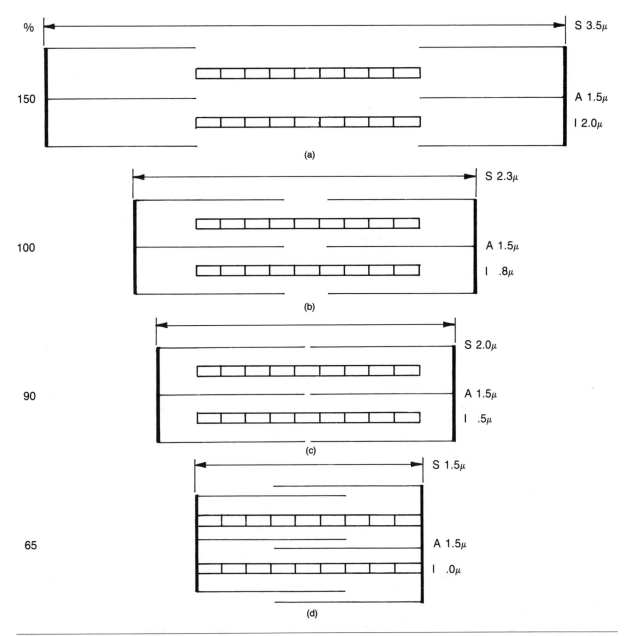

Figure 2. The lengthening and shortening of the sarcomere. (a) Stretched to approximately 150% of rest length, (b) at rest, 100% of rest length, (c) contracted to approximately 90% of rest length, and (d) contracted to approximately 65% of rest length. Sarcomere lengths (S) and A and I band lengths are given to the right of the diagrams. Lengths of sarcomeres expressed on % of rest length are given to the left. *Note.* From *Science of Stretching* (p. 18) by Michael J. Alter, 1988, Champaign, IL: Human Kinetics. Copyright 1988 by Michael J. Alter. Reprinted by permission.

to the muscle fiber. Because they are enclosed in the fusiform-shaped (i.e., tapering toward each end) spindle, they are referred to as *"intrafusal"* muscle fibers. The Golgi tendon organs (GTOs) are located in the tendons near the ends of the muscle fiber. Both of these are essentially stretch receptors. The muscle spindles respond to both changes in muscle length and the rate

(speed) of those changes of length, and the GTOs signal muscle force or tension.

The Stretch Reflex

The *stretch reflex* is a basic operation of the nervous system that helps maintain muscle tone and prevent injury. The stretch reflex

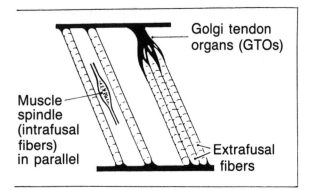

Figure 3. Fundamental difference in relations of muscle spindles and Golgi tendon organs to the extrafusal muscle fibers. *Note.* Reprinted from PHYSICAL THERAPY (Vol. 45: page 296, 1965) with the permission of the American Physical Therapy Association.

is initiated whenever a muscle is stretched. Stretching a muscle lengthens both the muscle fibers (i.e., the *extrafusal* fibers) and the muscle spindles, and this change in shape of the muscle spindles results in the firing of the stretch reflex: The muscle that is being stretched *contracts*.

The classic example of the stretch reflex is the knee jerk, or patella reflex. When the patella (kneecap) tendon is given a light tap, the muscle spindles that run parallel to the muscle fibers are stretched and change shape, causing the muscle spindles to fire. This sends a message to the spinal cord and brain. Completing the reflex arc, the spinal cord sends an impulse to the quadriceps (i.e., thigh muscles) and causes them to contract; the quadriceps shorten, and this takes the tension off the muscle spindles.

It is for this reason that you should generally avoid ballistic or bouncing types of stretches. A bouncing stretch makes muscular tension increase in the very muscle you are attempting to stretch, which makes it more difficult to stretch out the connective tissues. For the most effective stretching, the parts of the muscle that perform contraction must be totally relaxed. Therefore, stretching should be *slow* or *static*.

Reciprocal Innervation

Muscles usually operate in pairs, so that when one set of muscles, *agonistic*, is contracting, the opposing *antagonistic* muscles are relaxing. This grouping of coordinated

and opposing agonistic and antagonistic muscles is called *reciprocal innervation*. For example, when you flex your arm at the elbow by contracting your biceps, your triceps muscle, which normally extends the arm at the elbow, must relax. If it didn't, the two muscles would be pulling against each other, preventing movement. Similarly, the biceps muscle must relax when you attempt to extend your arm.

Reciprocal innervation is accomplished by cooperation brought about between the nerves supplying any antagonistic pair of muscles. When one of the pair receives an impulse to contract, the other relaxes because it does not receive an impulse to cause contraction. It is therefore *inhibited* at the same time that its opposing muscle contracts. However, it should be pointed out that such reciprocal inhibition is *not* obligatory. As a matter of fact, co-contraction could also occur.

By taking advantage of this phenomenon you can induce relaxation in the muscles you want to stretch. For example, to stretch your hamstrings, contract your quadriceps while in a modified hurdler's stretch; reciprocal innervation will make your hamstrings relax.

The Inverse Myotatic Reflex

Perhaps you have experienced a sudden, involuntary muscle relaxation when stretching. This is due to the *inverse myotatic reflex*. The Golgi tendon organs (GTOs) are thought to be responsible for this reflex. Other names for this phenomenon are *autogenic inhibition*, *lengthening reaction*, or *clasped-knife reflex*.

The GTOs operate in the following manner. When the intensity of a muscular contraction or stretch on a tendon exceeds a certain critical point, an immediate reflex occurs to inhibit the muscular contraction. As a result, the muscle immediately relaxes, and the excessive tension is removed. This reaction is possible only because the impulses of the GTOs are powerful enough to override the excitatory impulses of the muscle spindles. This relaxation is a protective mechanism—a safety device to prevent tendons and muscles from being injured by tearing away from their attachments.

The inverse myotatic reflex has two important implications for stretching. First, it may explain why, when an athlete is attempting to maintain a stretching position that develops considerable tension in the muscle, a point is suddenly reached where the tension dissipates and the muscle can be stretched even further. Second, by using a stretching strategy called the *contract-relax* technique (explained in a later section) relaxation can be induced in muscles that are being stretched. For example, stretch a limb or muscle to the point where further motion in the desired direction is prevented by the tension of the antagonist muscle. At this point, stretching against a partner, gradually build to a maximum contraction in the muscles for 5 to 15 seconds. This will cause the GTOs to fire and initiate the inverse myotatic reflex. Then move the joint through the gained range of joint motion. (Note, however, that there is a greater risk associated with this procedure because it develops more tension in the muscle, which may result in possible soreness and injury.)

HOW CONNECTIVE TISSUES ARE STRUCTURED

Connective tissue is the most abundant tissue in the body. It binds together and gives support to the various structures of the body. Its other functions include defense, protection, storage, transportation, and general support and repair. Obviously, then, connective tissue is extremely important for the athlete.

There are two types of connective tissue that most significantly affect an athlete's range of motion: *collagenous connective tissue* and *elastic connective tissue*. The former is composed primarily of collagen and the latter of elastic tissue. An athlete's range of motion is a combined result of blending and integrating these two tissues. Where collagenous fibers dominate, range of motion is restricted. Conversely, a dominance of elastic fibers allows a greater range of motion.

Connective tissues are comprised of progressively smaller units, including tendons, ligaments, and fascia. *Tendons* attach muscles to bones (see Figure 4a). *Ligaments* bind bones to bones. Technically, the term

fascia designates all fibrous connective tissues not otherwise specifically named.

The fascia that envelop and bind down muscle fibers into separate groups are named according to where they are found. These sheaths are the *endomysium*, *perimysium*, and *epimysium* (see Figure 4b). A muscle's resistance to stretch originates in the meshwork of these connective tissues; as you stretch, your connective tissues become more taut.

A question of great interest to all athletes is the relative importance of various tissues in joint stiffness. The joint capsule (i.e., the saclike structure that encloses the ends of bones) and ligaments are the most important factors, accounting for 47 percent of the stiffness, followed by the muscle's fascia (41 percent), the tendons (10 percent), and the skin (2 percent). However, most efforts to increase flexibility through stretching should be directed to the muscle fascia. The reasons for this are twofold. First, muscle and its fascia have more elastic tissue, so they are more modifiable in terms of reducing resistance to elongation. Second, because ligaments and tendons have less elasticity than fascia, it is undesirable to produce too much slack in them. Overstretching these structures may weaken the integrity of the joints. As a result, an excessive amount of flexibility may destabilize the joints and *increase* an athlete's risk of injury.

Because the connective tissues probably play the largest role in limiting an athlete's range of motion, they must be stretched properly, with the muscle relaxed to develop optimal flexibility.

HOW BONES AND JOINTS ARE STRUCTURED

Ultimately, an athlete's range of motion at a joint is restricted by both the bone and the joint structure. Just as the railroad track determines the route available to the train, so the shape and contour of the joint surfaces ultimately determine the movement pathways available to bones. Obviously, these pathways are further influenced by cartilage, ligaments, tendons, and other connective tissues that frequently serve as restraining factors.

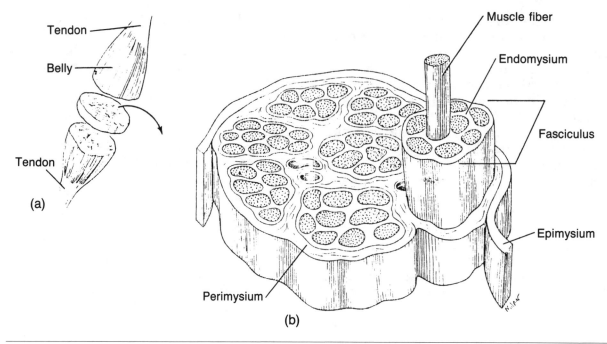

Figure 4. Connective tissue of a muscle. (a) Entire muscle, with the belly sectioned. (b) Enlargement of a cross section of the belly. *Note.* From *Human Anatomy and Physiology* (3rd ed., p. 215) by A.P. Spence and E.B. Mason, 1987, Menlo Park, CA: Benjamin/Cummings. Reprinted by permission.

The pelvic region exemplifies the correlation between joint structure and range of movement (see Figure 5a, b). The female pelvis allows a greater range of flexibility than the male. Some of the structural characteristics of the female pelvis that distinguish it from the male pelvis are these:

- Bones are lighter and smoother.
- Brim is round.
- Cavity is shallower and more capacious.
- Outlet is larger.
- Sacrosciatic notch is wider.
- Acetabula are further apart.
- Pubic arch is wider.
- Sacrum is wider and more curved.

WHAT HAPPENS WHEN YOU STRETCH

Several types of adaptation result from proper and regular stretching. First, as we pointed out earlier, when a muscle is suddenly stretched, the stretch reflex is initiated and the muscle being stretched contracts. However, through training, the critical point at which the stretch reflex is initiated can be "reset" to a higher level. Consequently, your muscles relax farther into the stretch.

Second, with increased stretching over a period of time the fascial sheaths encasing your muscles may undergo semipermanent change in length. These sheaths would include the epimysium, endomysium, and perimysium (see Figure 4b). Additional tissues adapting to the stretch would be the tendons, ligaments, fascia, and scar tissues.

Lastly, stretching is thought to stimulate the production and retention of gel-like substances called *glycoaminoglycans* (GAGs). The GAGs, along with water and hyaluronic acid, lubricate connective tissue fibers, maintaining a critical distance between them. This prevents the fibers from touching one another and sticking together. As a result, excessive cross-linkages are not formed (see Figure 6).

DIFFERENT METHODS OF STRETCHING

Just as in the proverbial "there is more than one way to skin a cat," there is also more than one way to stretch your muscles.

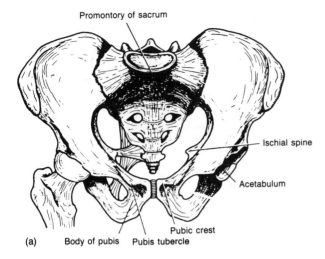

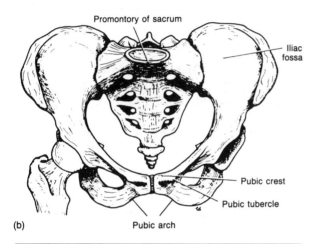

Figure 5. The male pelvis (a) and the female pelvis (b). *Note.* From *Clinical Anatomy for Medical Students* (3rd ed., p. 304) by R.S. Snell, 1986, Boston: Little, Brown and Company. Copyright 1986 by Little, Brown and Company. Reprinted by permission.

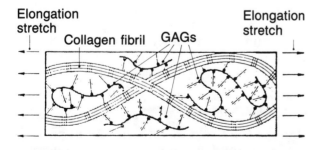

Figure 6. The action of GAGs. Stretch is applied to collagen fibrils, but the GAGs keep the fibrils separated and aligned. *Note.* Reprinted by permission of VCH Publishers, Inc., 220 East 23rd St., New York, N.Y., 10010. From: Hukins: *Connective Tissue Matrix*, 1984.

Stretching refers to the process of elongation. Stretching exercises are performed in a variety of ways depending upon your goals, abilities, and state of training. For example, a world-class gymnast or black belt in karate should perform more advanced stretches than individuals who are beginning stretching programs simply to improve their personal health and fitness. There are five basic stretching techniques: static, ballistic, passive, active, and proprioceptive.

Static Stretching

Static stretching involves holding a position. That is, you stretch to the farthest point and hold the stretch. Splits are a good example of static stretching. The most important advantage of static stretching is that it is the *safest* method of stretching. Other advantages include these:

- It requires little expenditure of energy.
- It allows adequate time to reset the sensitivity of the stretch reflex.
- It permits semipermanent change in length.
- It can induce muscular relaxation via the firing of the GTOs if the stretch is held long enough.

Ballistic Stretching

Ballistic stretching involves bobbing, bouncing, rebounding, and rhythmic types of movements. This technique is the most controversial stretching method because it can cause the most soreness and injury. Other disadvantages are these:

- It fails to provide adequate time for the tissues to adapt to the stretch.
- It initiates the stretch reflex and thereby increases muscular tension, making it more difficult to stretch out the connective tissues.
- It does not provide adequate time for neurological adaptation (i.e., of the stretch reflex) to take place.

Despite these disadvantages, there are several reasons why some athletes might use ballistic stretching exercises. This method is effective for developing flexibility. More importantly, in terms of specificity of training it is appropriate for developing dynamic flexibility (movement due to momentum); this is essential for certain events and sports, such as ballet and karate. Subjectively, ballistic stretching can be less boring than other stretching methods.

Passive Stretching

Passive stretching is a technique in which you are relaxed and make no contribution to the range of motion. Instead, an external force is created by an outside agent, either manually or mechanically. Among the advantages associated with passive stretching are these:

- It is effective when the agonist (the primary muscle responsible for the movement) is too weak to respond.
- It is effective when attempts to inhibit the tight muscles (i.e., the antagonists) are unsuccessful.
- It allows stretching beyond one's active range of motion.
- Direction, duration, and intensity can be measured when more advanced stretching machines and modalities are used in rehabilitative therapy.
- It can promote team comradery when athletes stretch with partners.

The major disadvantage associated with passive stretching is its greater risk of resulting in soreness and injury if a partner applies the external force incorrectly. In addition, it may initiate the stretch reflex if the stretch is too rapid, and the likelihood of injury increases with greater differences between the ranges of active and passive flexibility. But the solution here is to also develop your active flexibility.

Active Stretching

Active stretching is accomplished using your own muscles and without any assistance from an external force. An example of active stretching is standing upright and slowly lifting one leg to a 45-degree angle. Active stretching is important because it develops active flexibility, which in turn has been found to have a higher correlation with sports achievement than does passive flexibility. The major disadvantages of active stretching are that it may initiate the stretch reflex and that it may be ineffective in the presence of certain dysfunctions and injuries such as severe sprains, inflammation, or fractures.

Proprioceptive Neuromuscular Facilitation

Proprioceptive neuromuscular facilitation (PNF) is another broad strategy that can be implemented to improve your range of motion. This technique is also referred to in certain disciplines as a *muscle energy technique.* PNF was originally designed and developed as a physical therapy procedure for the rehabilitation of patients. Today, several different types of PNF are being used in the arena of sports medicine. Two of the most prevalent are the contract-relax technique and the contract-relax-contract technique.

Contract-Relax Technique (Hold-Relax)

The contract-relax technique starts with the athlete's *tight* muscle group in a lengthened position. Assume for the sake of illustration that your hamstrings are tight. The tight hamstrings are first placed under a gentle stretch and then gradually contract isometrically, building to a maximum effort for 6 to 15 seconds against the resistance of your partner. There is no change in the muscle's length or movement of the joint. This is followed by a brief period of relaxing the hamstrings. Then your partner slowly lengthens the tight muscle group by passively moving the extremity through its gained range of motion.

Contract-Relax-Contract Technique (Hold-Relax-Contract)

The contract-relax-contract technique is similar to the contract-relax technique except that after the relaxation phase you *actively contract* the agonist (i.e., the antagonist of the tight muscle group, which in this instance is your quadriceps). This last phase can also be assisted by the partner. Then the entire procedure is repeated.

PNF techniques are claimed to offer a wider range of advantages and benefits over other conventional stretching methods. Most significantly, it is claimed to be the most successful method for developing flexibility. PNF is also praised because it enhances active flexibility and helps establish a pattern for coordinated motion. The technique is also considered superior because it uses several important neurophysiological mechanisms. These include such things as reciprocal innervation and the inverse myotatic reflex. For example, PNF techniques may help reset the stretch reflex level and promote relaxation in the muscles to be stretched.

Unfortunately, PNF techniques have several disadvantages. Most important is the greater risk of injury, ranging from a pulled muscle to certain cardiovascular complications. Furthermore, this technique requires a knowledgeable and well-trained partner.

WHAT CAUSES MUSCULAR SORENESS

Athletes commonly experience discomfort, soreness, stiffness, or pain. These afflictions fall into two general categories: those that occur during and immediately after the exercise or stretching (these may persist for several hours), and those that usually do not appear until 24 to 48 hours later. Currently, there are four basic hypotheses that attempt to explain the nature of muscular soreness:

- The torn tissue hypothesis
- The connective tissue damage hypothesis
- The metabolic accumulation hypothesis
- The localized spasm of motor units hypothesis

Although these will be analyzed separately, they can occur together. It is also possible that there are other causes of muscular soreness.

Torn Tissue or Connective Tissue Damage

One explanation for muscular soreness is the *torn tissue hypothesis*. This hypothesis is that soreness results from the microscopic tearing of muscle fibers or connective tissues. More recently, this has been expanded into the *connective tissue damage hypothesis*, which suggests that the soreness is due to irritation or damage of connective tissue—usually a result of exercises or training that utilize eccentric contractions (for instance, the elongation or stretching of a muscle while it is contracting under a resistance). *Plyometrics* is an example of a training technique that utilizes eccentric contractions.

Metabolic Accumulation or Osmotic Pressure and Swelling

A popular explanation of immediate muscle soreness is the *metabolic accumulation* or *osmotic pressure and swelling hypothesis*, which suggests that the accumulation of waste products, especially lactic acid, is the chief culprit. Another explanation is that an excessive accumulation of metabolites causes an increased osmotic pressure: Pressure on the athlete's sensory nerves creates the pain.

Localized Spasm of Motor Units

The *localized spasm of motor units hypothesis*, developed by de Vries, is intended to explain delayed localized soreness. By this hypothesis, exercise above a minimal level causes decreased blood flow to the muscle, or *ischemia*, which in turn causes pain that results in a protective, reflex, tonic muscle contraction. The tonic contraction brings about more ischemia, and a vicious cycle is born.

An important thing to remember is that some degree of soreness is often experienced by those who have not previously exercised or stretched—this is the penalty for having been inactive. On the other hand, well-trained athletes who work out at higher-than-usual levels of difficulty can also become sore. (However, you should immediately stop exercising if you feel or hear something popping or tearing.) As a general rule, remember the acronym *RICE* when treating an injured body part:

- Rest
- Ice
- Compression
- Elevation

This will help to minimize the pain and swelling. Then seek appropriate professional advice.

HOW AGING AFFECTS FLEXIBILITY

Flexibility can be developed at any age given the appropriate training. However, the rate of development will not be the same at every age for all athletes. Generally speaking, small children are quite supple, and flexibility increases during the school years. With the onset of adolescence, flexibility tends to level off and then begins to decrease.

The primary factor responsible for the decline of flexibility with age is certain changes that occur in the connective tissues of the body. Interestingly, it has been suggested that exercise can delay the loss of flexibility due to the aging process of dehydration. This is based on the notion that stretching stimulates the production or retention of lubricants between the connective tissue fibers, thus preventing the formation of adhesions. Among the physical changes associated with aging are these:

- An increased amount of calcium deposits
- An increased degree of dehydration
- An increased level of fragmentation
- An increased number of adhesions and cross-links
- An actual change in the chemical structure of the tissues
- The replacement of muscle fibers with fatty and fibrous (collagen) fibers

WARMING UP

The warm-up is an essential part of a good conditioning program. It consists of a group of exercises performed immediately before an activity and provides an athlete with a period of adjustment from rest to exercise. These exercises are designed to improve performance and reduce the chance of injury by mobilizing the athlete mentally as well as physically. In contrast, flexibility or stretching exercises are those used to increase range of motion progressively and permanently. Stretching should always be preceded by a warm-up.

Warm-up routines are typically classified into three categories. A *passive* warm-up involves raising the body temperature by some external means such as heating pads and hot showers. A *general* warm-up is probably the most commonly used technique. It employs various movements not directly related to those employed in the activity itself. These include light calisthenics, brisk walking, jogging, or jumping rope. A *formal* or *specific* warm-up includes movements that either mimic or are employed in the actual activity, performed at a reduced level of intensity.

Benefits of a Good Warm-Up

- Increase in body and tissue temperature
- Increase of blood flow through the active muscles
- Increase in heart rate, which prepares the cardiovascular system for work
- Increase in rate at which energy is released in the body (i.e., the metabolic rate)
- Increase in the exchange of oxygen from hemoglobin
- Increase in speed at which nerve impulses travel, facilitating body movements
- Increase in efficiency in the process of reciprocal innervation (thus allowing muscles to contract and relax faster and more efficiently)
- Increase in physical work capacity
- Decrease in muscular tension
- Enhancement of the ability of connective tissue to elongate
- Enhancement of the athlete psychologically

The intensity and duration of a warm-up must be suited to the athlete's physical capabilities and adjusted to the existing conditions. Generally speaking, an athlete's warm-up should be intense enough to increase the body temperature and cause some sweating but not so intense as to cause fatigue. A warm-up in cold weather should be more intense.

THE CONTROVERSY ABOUT STRETCHING

Stretching exercises should not be considered a panacea. For some athletes stretching may actually increase the likelihood of ligament injury and joint separation or dislocation! The basis of this claim is that excessive flexibility may destabilize the athlete's joints. Some experts also feel that excessively loose joints may lead to premature development of osteoarthritis in athletes.

What, then, are the precautions for stretching, and when should it be considered inadvisable? The most commonly cited precautions are listed in the following box.*

Don't stretch if . . .

. . . a bone blocks motion.
. . . you've had a recent fracture of a bone.
. . . an acute inflammatory or infectious process in or around a joint is suspected or known.
. . . osteoporosis is suspected or known.
. . . there is sharp, acute pain with joint movement or muscle elongation.
. . . you've had a recent sprain or strain.
. . . you suffer from certain vascular or skin diseases.
. . . there is a loss of function or decrease in range of motion.

---

*The precautions are matters of medical/professional *opinions*, not established fact. Therefore, they are controversial. Whenever in doubt, seek professional advice!

"X-RATED" EXERCISES

Virtually every stretch presents some degree of risk. The possibility of an injury depends upon numerous variables, including an athlete's state of training, age, previous injuries, structural abnormalities, fatigue, and improper technique.

The stretches listed here are rated "X". By this, we mean they are in all likelihood too advanced or dangerous for the lay public just starting on an exercise program—and, perhaps, for advanced athletes as well. Needless to say, many of these and other stretches are considered an integral part of dance, gymnastics, the martial arts, wrestling, and yoga.

The Plough

- Places excessive strain on the lower back and is potentially dangerous for those with lower back problems
- Places excessive pressure on the discs
- Stretches a region that frequently tends to be flexed from faulty posture
- Compresses the lungs and heart
- Interferes with breathing if there is an excessive deposit of fat about the abdominal region

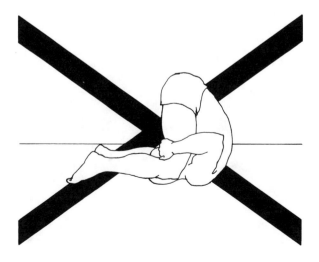

The Single- or Double-Leg Inverted Hurdler's Stretch

- Stretches the medial ligaments of the knee
- Crushes the meniscus
- Promotes knee instability
- Twists and compresses the kneecap, resulting in its side-slipping

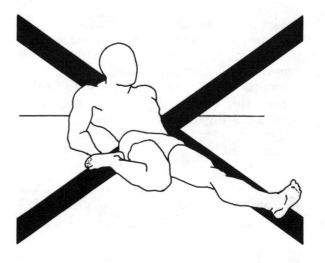

The Deep Knee Bend/Lunge/Squat (with or without weights)

- Endangers the lateral ligaments of the knee
- Compresses the kneecap
- Pinches and damages the cartilage

The Standing Torso Twist (with or without weights)

- Can strain the ligaments of the knee
- Uses momentum that often exceeds the absorbing capacity of the tissues being stretched

The Straight-Leg Straddle Stand and Floor/Toe Touch

- Stresses the medial aspect of the knees
- Can result in permanent deformity, both as loose and knocked knees
- Forces the knees to hyperextend
- Places greater pressure on the lumbar vertebrae

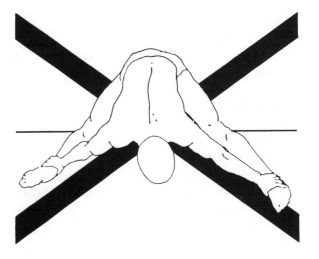

The Straight-Leg Standing Floor/Toe Touch

- Forces the knees to hyperextend
- Places greater pressure on the lower (lumbar) vertebrae

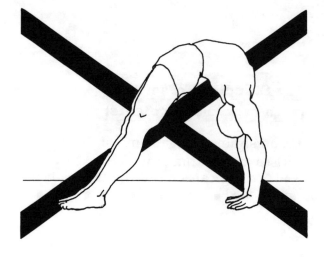

The Bridge

- Squeezes the spinal discs
- Pinches the nerve fibers

Inversion

- Raises blood pressure
- May rupture blood vessels—especially in the eyes
- May injure those with spinal instability

STRETCHING ROUTINES FOR SPECIFIC SPORTS

Ideally, stretching routines should be tailored to your needs. The tables in this section suggest routines that will cover virtually your entire body. If each stretch is held for 30 seconds it should take 15 to 20 minutes to perform all of the stretches in each table. The exercises are numbered in order of their appearance of Part III.

Additionally, the most beneficial stretches for each sport are illustrated, and beneath each figure is the number that coincides with the stretch. The number will help you find the description and instructions for the stretch in Part III. If you find the stretches either too easy or difficult, simply substitute another that meets your needs for the same muscle group or region.

In closing, if you are truly a serious athlete the 20 minutes spent on stretching may be the most important minutes of your practice or performance session. The time spent must be thought of as "triple A" investment in your most valuable asset—your body. Remember, *your body is your instrument.*

PART II

PRESTRETCHING GUIDELINES

Follow these guidelines before beginning a stretching program.

- See a physician and take a medical examination before beginning any exercise program.
- Always make sure safety comes first. Everyone must be involved in the prevention of injuries.
- Identify specific and realistic goals.
- Do not stretch immediately before eating.
- Empty your bladder and bowels before stretching.
- Wear loose and comfortable clothes.
- Remove all jewelry.
- Discard all candy and gum.
- Select a clean and quiet place to stretch.
- Work on a nonskid surface—preferably a firm mat.

STRETCHING GUIDELINES

Before beginning a stretching routine, always follow these guidelines.

- Warm up prior to stretching.
- Develop a positive mental attitude.
- Isolate the muscle group to be stretched.
- Move slowly and smoothly into the stretch to avoid initiation of the stretch reflex.
- Use proper mechanics and strive for correct alignment.
- Breathe normally and freely, but accentuate the exhalation when moving deeper into the stretch.
- Hold the stretch (usually about 20 seconds to 1 minute) and relax. Do *not* strain or passively force a joint beyond its normal range of motion.
- Concentrate and feel the stretch.
- Anticipate and communicate when stretching with a partner.
- Come out of each stretch as carefully as you went into it.

BASEBALL

Stretching Routine for Baseball (General)					
Body part	*Stretch number*	*Body part*	*Stretch number*	*Body part*	*Stretch number*
Plantar arch	2, 4	Hip flexors	135-137, **144-145**	Chest/pectoralis	254, 257, **261**
Anterior toes	5	Buttocks & hips	152-153, 157, 159, 162, **170, 172**	Anterior shoulder	264-265, **268-270**
Ankles/Anterior lower leg	7, 11	Abdomen & hips	178-179, **195**	Lateral shoulder	271
Ankles/Lateral lower leg	13, 19	Lower back	198, 200, **201**, 205, 207	Internal rotators	273, **277**, 278
Achilles tendon	25, **28***, 30, 32	Lateral trunk	221-222, **229**, 230	External rotators	**282**, 284-285
Back of knee	45	Upper back	234	Shoulder flexors	286, **291**
Hamstrings	53, 55, **67**, 75	Posterior neck	237, 242, **247**	Biceps	296
Adductors	87, 91-92, 96, **105**	Lateral neck	250	Triceps	299, 301, **303**
Quadriceps	121, 123 127, **129**	Anterior neck	252	Wrist extensors	305-306
				Wrist flexors	308-310

*Boldfaced numbers indicate partner stretches.

Most Beneficial Stretches for Baseball Players

13   25   55   91   127   137

157   178   230   264   284   299

BASEBALL

Stretching Routine for Baseball (Pitcher)					
Body part	*Stretch number*	*Body part*	*Stretch number*	*Body part*	*Stretch number*
Plantar arch	2-3	Hip flexors	136	Chest/ pectoralis	257, 259
Anterior toes	5	Buttocks & hips	152, 158, 160	Anterior shoulder	265-266
Ankles/Anterior lower leg	7-8	Abdomen & hips	179, 182	Lateral shoulder	271
Ankles/Lateral lower leg	13, 15	Lower back	198, 203, 205	Internal rotators	274, 278, 284-285
Achilles tendon	25, 31	Lateral trunk	221-223	External rotators	279-280, 284-285
Back of knee	45	Upper back	234	Shoulder flexors Biceps	286 295-296
Hamstrings	53, 55, 74	Posterior neck	237-238	Triceps	299-300
Adductors	92, 97, 102	Lateral neck	249-250	Wrist extensors	305-307
Quadriceps	123-126	Anterior neck	252	Wrist flexors	308-310

Most Beneficial Stretches for Pitchers

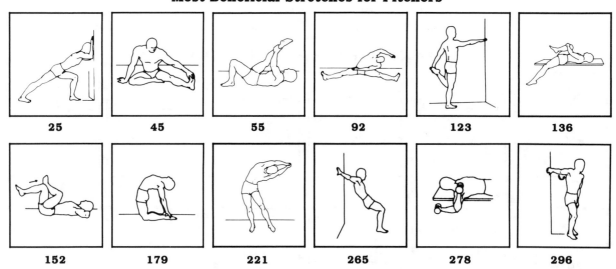

25   45   55   92   123   136

152   179   221   265   278   296

BASKETBALL

Stretching Routine for Basketball

Body part	Stretch number	Body part	Stretch number	Body part	Stretch number
Plantar arch	3-4	Hip flexors	135-137, **144-145**	Chest/pectoralis	254, 257, **261**
Anterior toes	5	Buttocks & hips	151-153, 159, 161-162, **170, 172**	Anterior shoulder	264-265, **268-270**
Ankles/Anterior lower leg	7, 11	Abdomen & hips	178-179, 181, **195**	Lateral shoulder	271
Ankles/Lateral lower leg	13, 19	Lower back	198, 200, **201**, 205, 207	Internal rotators	273, **277**
Achilles tendon	25, **28***, 30-32	Lateral trunk	221-222, **229**	External rotators	**282**, 284-285
Back of knee	45	Upper back	234	Shoulder flexors	286, **291**
				Biceps	296
Hamstrings	53, 55, **67**	Posterior neck	237, 242, **247**	Triceps	299-301, **303**
Adductors	87, 96, **105**	Lateral neck	250	Wrist extensors	305-306
Quadriceps	121, 123, **129**	Anterior neck	252	Wrist flexors	308-310

*Boldfaced numbers indicate partner stretches.

Most Beneficial Stretches for Basketball Players

3 13 55 87 121 151

161 181 221 271 286 300

BICYCLING

Stretching Routine for Bicycling					
Body part	*Stretch number*	*Body part*	*Stretch number*	*Body part*	*Stretch number*
Plantar arch	4	Hip flexors	135-137, **144-145**	Chest/ pectoralis	254, 257, **261**
Anterior toes	5	Buttocks & hips	152-153, 159, 162, **170, 172**	Anterior shoulder	264-265, **268-270**
Ankles/Anterior lower leg	7, 11	Abdomen & hips	178-179, 184-185, **195**	Lateral shoulder	271
Ankles/Lateral lower leg	13, 19	Lower back	198, 200, **201**, 202, 205, 207	Internal rotators	273, **277**
Achilles tendon	25, **28***, 30, 32	Lateral trunk	221-222, **229**	External rotators	**282**, 284-285
Back of knee	45	Upper back	234	Shoulder flexors	286, **291**
Hamstrings	53, 55, **67**, 72	Posterior neck	237, 242, **247**	Biceps	296
Adductors	87, 95-96, **105**	Lateral neck	250	Triceps	299, 301, **303**
Quadriceps	121, 123, 126, **129**, 134	Anterior neck	252	Wrist extensors	305-306
				Wrist flexors	308-310

*Boldfaced numbers indicate partner stretches.

Most Beneficial Stretches for Bicyclists

32   53   87   95   126   134

136   159   179   202   237   250

BOWLING

Stretching Routine for Bowling					
Body part	*Stretch number*	*Body part*	*Stretch number*	*Body part*	*Stretch number*
Plantar arch	4	Hip flexors	135-137, **144-145**	Chest/ pectoralis	254, 257, **261**
Anterior toes	6	Buttocks & hips	152-153, 155 159, 162, **170, 172**	Anterior shoulder	264-265, **268-270**
Ankles/Anterior lower leg	7, 11	Abdomen & hips	178-179, **195**	Lateral shoulder	271
Ankles/Lateral lower leg	13, 18-19	Lower back	198, 200, **201**, 205, 207	Internal rotators	273, **277**
Achilles tendon	25, **28***, 30, 32, 36	Lateral trunk	215, 221-222, **229**	External rotators	**282**, 284-285
Back of knee	45	Upper back	234	Shoulder flexors	286, **291**
Hamstrings	53, 55, **67**, 73	Posterior neck	237, 242, **247**	Biceps	296
Adductors	87, 96-97, **105**	Lateral neck	250	Triceps	299-301, **303**
Quadriceps	121, 123-125, **129**	Anterior neck	252	Wrist extensors	305-306
				Wrist flexors	308-311
*Boldfaced numbers indicate partner stretches.					

Most Beneficial Stretches for Bowlers

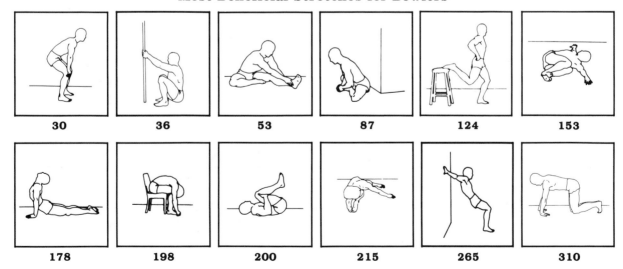

30   36   53   87   124   153

178   198   200   215   265   310

DANCE

Stretching Routine for Dance					
Body part	*Stretch number*	*Body part*	*Stretch number*	*Body part*	*Stretch number*
Plantar arch	1, 4	Hip flexors	135-137, **144, 146-147**	Chest/ pectoralis	254, 257, **261**
Anterior toes	5-6	Buttocks & hips	151-153, 159, 168, **170, 172**	Anterior shoulder	264-265, **268-270**
Ankles/Anterior lower leg	7-8, 11	Abdomen & hips	179, 188, 191-192, **195**	Lateral shoulder	271
Ankles/Lateral lower leg	13, 19	Lower back	198, 200, **201**, 206-207	Internal rotators	273, **277**
Achilles tendon	25, **28***, 30, 32-33, 37-41	Lateral trunk	221-222, **229**	External rotators	280, **282**, 284-285
Back of knee	45	Upper back	234	Shoulder flexors	286-287, **289, 291, 293**
Hamstrings	53, 59, 61, 63, **67-68**	Posterior neck	245-246, **247**	Biceps	296
Adductors	96, 99, 103-104, **116**	Lateral neck	250	Triceps	299, 301, **303**
Quadriceps	123, 128, **129**, 138-139	Anterior neck	252	Wrist extensors	305-306
				Wrist flexors	308-310

*Boldfaced numbers indicate partner stretches.

Most Beneficial Stretches for Dancers

1   37   61   99   104   128

147   151   188   221   280   301

DIVING

Stretching Routine for Diving					
Body part	*Stretch number*	*Body part*	*Stretch number*	*Body part*	*Stretch number*
Plantar arch	4	Hip flexors	135-137, **144-145**	Chest/ pectoralis	254, 257, **261**
Anterior toes	5-6	Buttocks & hips	152-154, 159, 162, **170, 172**	Anterior shoulder	264-265, **268-270**
Ankles/Anterior lower leg	7-12	Abdomen & hips	178-179, **195**	Lateral shoulder	271
Ankles/Lateral lower leg	13, 19	Lower back	198, 200, **201**, 205-207	Internal rotators	273, **277**
Achilles tendon	25, **28***, 30, 32	Lateral trunk	221-222, **229**	External rotators	**282**, 284-285
Back of knee	45, 52	Upper back	234	Shoulder flexors	286, **291**, **293**
Hamstrings	53, 55, **67** 71, 77-79	Posterior neck	237, 242, **247**	Biceps	296
Adductors	87, 91, 96, **105**	Lateral neck	250	Triceps	299, 301, **303**
Quadriceps	123, **129**, 134	Anterior neck	252	Wrist extensors	305-306
				Wrist flexors	308-310

*Boldfaced numbers indicate partner stretches.

Most Beneficial Stretches for Divers

8   32   45   71   79   91

134   154   179   206   234   301

FOOTBALL

Stretching Routine for Football					
Body part	*Stretch number*	*Body part*	*Stretch number*	*Body part*	*Stretch number*
Plantar arch	2-4	Hip flexors	135-137, **144-145**	Chest/ pectoralis	254-257, **261**
Anterior toes	5	Buttocks & hips	150, 152-153, 159, 162, 167, **170, 172**	Anterior shoulder	264-265, **268-270**
Ankles/Anterior lower leg	7-8, 11	Abdomen & hips	178-179, **195**	Lateral shoulder	271
Ankles/Lateral lower leg	13-15, 19	Lower back	198-200, **201**, 204-205, 207	Internal rotators	273, **277**
Achilles tendon	22, 25, **28***, 30, 32	Lateral trunk	218, 221-222, **229**	External rotators	**282**, 284-285
Back of knee	45	Upper back	234	Shoulder flexors	286, **291**
Hamstrings	53-55, **67**, 74	Posterior neck	237, 242, **247**	Biceps	296
Adductors	87, 91, 96, 102, **105**	Lateral neck	250	Triceps	299, 301, **303**
Quadriceps	122-123, **129**	Anterior neck	252	Wrist extensors	305-306
				Wrist flexors	308-310

*Boldfaced numbers indicate partner stretches.

Most Beneficial Stretches for Football Players

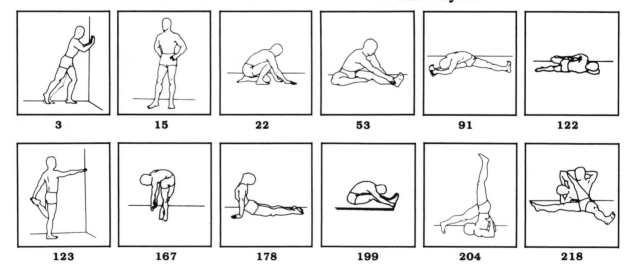

3   15   22   53   91   122

123   167   178   199   204   218

GOLF

Stretching Routine for Golf					
Body part	*Stretch number*	*Body part*	*Stretch number*	*Body part*	*Stretch number*
Plantar arch	4	Hip flexors	135-137, **144-145**	Chest/ pectoralis	254, 257, **261**
Anterior toes	5	Buttocks & hips	150-154, 159, 162-163, **170, 172**	Anterior shoulder	264-265, **268-270**
Ankles/Anterior lower leg	7, 11	Abdomen & hips	178-179, **195**	Lateral shoulder	271
Ankles/Lateral lower leg	13, 18-19	Lower back	198, 200, **201**, 205, 207	Internal rotators	273, **277**
Achilles tendon	21, 25, **28***, 30, 32	Lateral trunk	221-222, **229**	External rotators	**282**, 284-285
Back of knee	45	Upper back	234	Shoulder flexors	286, **291**
Hamstrings	53-55, **67**	Posterior neck	237, 242, **247**	Biceps	296
Adductors	86-88, 96, **105**	Lateral neck	250	Triceps	299, 301, **303**
Quadriceps	121, 123, **129**, 131	Anterior neck	252	Wrist extensors	305-306
				Wrist flexors	308-310

*Boldfaced numbers indicate partner stretches.

Most Beneficial Stretches for Golfers

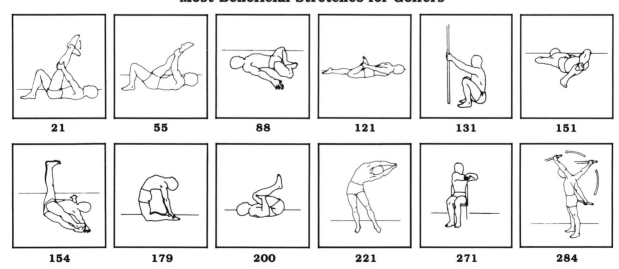

21   55   88   121   131   151

154   179   200   221   271   284

GYMNASTICS

Stretching Routine for Gymnastics

Body part	Stretch number	Body part	Stretch number	Body part	Stretch number
Plantar arch	4	Hip flexors	135-137, **144, 146-147**	Chest/ pectoralis	254, 257, **261**
Anterior toes	5-6	Buttocks & hips	151-153, 159, 162, **170, 172**	Anterior shoulder	264-265, 267, **268-270**
Ankles/Anterior lower leg	7-12	Abdomen & hips	178-179, 188-192, **195**	Lateral shoulder	271
Ankles/Lateral lower leg	13, 19	Lower back	198, 200, **201**, 206, 207	Internal rotators	273, **277**
Achilles tendon	24-26, **28***, 30, 32	Lateral trunk	223, **229**	External rotators	**282**, 284-285
Back of knee	45	Upper back	234	Shoulder flexors	286, 287, **289, 291, 293**
Hamstrings	53, 55, 61, 63, **67-68**	Posterior neck	244-246, **247**	Biceps	296
Adductors	87, 96 103-104, **116**	Lateral neck	250	Triceps	299, 301, **303**
Quadriceps	123, 128, **129**, 134, 138	Anterior neck	252	Wrist extensors	305-306
				Wrist flexors	308-310

*Boldfaced numbers indicate partner stretches.

Most Beneficial Stretches for Gymnasts

4   24   61   104   134   151

191   223   234   244   265   284

HANDBALL

Stretching Routine for Handball

Body part	Stretch number	Body part	Stretch number	Body part	Stretch number
Plantar arch	4	Hip flexors	135-137, **144-145**	Chest/ pectoralis	254, 257, **261**
Anterior toes	5	Buttocks & hips	152-153, 156, 159, 162, **170, 172**	Anterior shoulder	264-265, **268-270**
Ankles/Anterior lower leg	7, 11	Abdomen & hips	178-179, **195**	Lateral shoulder	271
Ankles/Lateral lower leg	13-14, 19	Lower back	198, 200, **201**, 202, 205, 207	Internal rotators	273, **277**
Achilles tendon	23, 25, 27, **28***, 30, 32	Lateral trunk	221-222, **229**	External rotators	**282**, 284-285
Back of knee	45	Upper back	234	Shoulder flexors	286, **291, 293**
Hamstrings	53, 55, **67**, 76	Posterior neck	237, 242, **247**	Biceps	296
Adductors	87, 92, 96-97, **105**	Lateral neck	250	Triceps	299, 301, **303**
Quadriceps	121, 123, **129**	Anterior neck	252	Wrist extensors	305-306
				Wrist flexors	308-310

*Boldfaced numbers indicate partner stretches.

Most Beneficial Stretches for Handball Players

4   7   11   23   55   92

121   156   178   202   271   301

HOCKEY

Stretching Routine for Hockey					
Body part	*Stretch number*	*Body part*	*Stretch number*	*Body part*	*Stretch number*
Plantar arch	4	Hip flexors	133, 135-137, **144-145**	Chest/ pectoralis	254, 257, **261**
Anterior toes	5	Buttocks & hips	152-153, 159, 162, **170, 172**	Anterior shoulder	264-265, **268-270**
Ankles/Anterior lower leg	7, 11	Abdomen & hips	178-179, **195**	Lateral shoulder	271
Ankles/Lateral lower leg	13, 19	Lower back	198, 200, **201**, 205, 207	Internal rotators	273, **277**
Achilles tendon	25, **28***, 30, 32	Lateral trunk	221-222, **229**, 230	External rotators	**282**, 284-285
Back of knee	45	Upper back	234	Shoulder flexors	286, **291, 293**
Hamstrings	53, 55, **67**	Posterior neck	237, 242, **247**	Biceps	296
Adductors	87, 94, 96, **105**	Lateral neck	250	Triceps	299, 301, **303**
Quadriceps	123, **129**	Anterior neck	252	Wrist extensors	305-306
				Wrist flexors	308-310

*Boldfaced numbers indicate partner stretches.

Most Beneficial Stretches for Hockey Players

7	30	53	87	96	133

137	179	230	264	271	284

JOGGING

Stretching Routine for Jogging					
Body part	*Stretch number*	*Body part*	*Stretch number*	*Body part*	*Stretch number*
Plantar arch	4	Hip flexors	135-137, **144-145**	Chest/ pectoralis	254, 257, **261**
Anterior toes	6	Buttocks & hips	152-153, 159, 162, 164, 167, **170, 172**	Anterior shoulder	264-265, **268-270**
Ankles/Anterior lower leg	7, 11	Abdomen & hips	178-179, **195**	Lateral shoulder	271
Ankles/Lateral lower leg	13-14, 19-20	Lower back	198, 200, **201**, 205, 207	Internal rotators	273, **277**
Achilles tendon	25-26, **28***, 30, 32	Lateral trunk	221-222, **229**, 230	External rotators	**282**, 284-285
Back of knee	45-46	Upper back	234	Shoulder flexors	286, **291, 293**
Hamstrings	53, 55, **67**, 72	Posterior neck	237, 242, **247**	Biceps	296
Adductors	87, 91, 94, 96, **105**	Lateral neck	250	Triceps	299, 301, **303**
Quadriceps	123, **129**	Anterior neck	252	Wrist extensors	305-306
				Wrist flexors	308-310
*Boldfaced numbers indicate partner stretches.					

Most Beneficial Stretches for Joggers

4   7   11   19   53   91

123   153   167   200   250   286

MARTIAL ARTS

Stretching Routine for Martial Arts (Beginning)					
Body part	*Stretch number*	*Body part*	*Stretch number*	*Body part*	*Stretch number*
Plantar arch	4	Hip flexors	135-137, **144-145**	Chest/pectoralis	254, 257, **261**
Anterior toes	6	Buttocks & hips	152-153, 159, 162, **170, 172-173**	Anterior shoulder	264-265, **268-270**
Ankles/Anterior lower leg	7, 11	Abdomen & hips	178-179, 188-189, **195**	Lateral shoulder	271
Ankles/Lateral lower leg	13, 19	Lower back	198, 200, **201**, 205-206	Internal rotators	273, **277**
Achilles tendon	23, 25, **28***, 30, 32	Lateral trunk	221, 223, **229**	External rotators	**282**, 284-285
Back of knee	45	Upper back	234	Shoulder flexors	286-287, **289, 291, 293**
Hamstrings	53, 55, 60, 62, 64, **67-70**	Posterior neck	239, 241, 244-246, **247**	Biceps	296
Adductors	87, 93, 96, 104, **116-117**	Lateral neck	250	Triceps	299, 301, **303**
Quadriceps	123, **129**, 134, 138	Anterior neck	252	Wrist extensors	305-306
				Wrist flexors	308-310

*Boldfaced numbers indicate partner stretches.

Most Beneficial Stretches for Beginning Martial Artists

23   60   62   64   96   104

134   137   162   179   205   221

MARTIAL ARTS

Stretching Routine for Martial Arts (Advanced)

Body part	Stretch number	Body part	Stretch number	Body part	Stretch number
Plantar arch	3	Hip flexors	**144-145, 147**	Chest/ pectoralis	**261**
Anterior toes	6	Buttocks & hips	**172-173**	Anterior shoulder	**269**
Ankles/Anterior lower leg	8, 11-12	Abdomen & hips	190, **195**	Lateral shoulder	**272**
Ankles/Lateral lower leg	15, 20	Lower back	211	Internal rotators	**277**
Achilles tendon	**28***	Lateral trunk	**229**	External rotators	**281-282**
Back of knee	51-52	Upper back	**235-236**	Shoulder flexors	**289, 293**
Hamstrings	60, 61, 64, **67-69**	Posterior neck	**248**	Biceps	296
Adductors	104, **112-113, 117**	Lateral neck	250	Triceps	**303**
Quadriceps	129, 139	Anterior neck	253	Wrist extensors	306
				Wrist flexors	310

*Boldfaced numbers indicate partner stretches.

Most Beneficial Stretches for Advanced Martial Artists

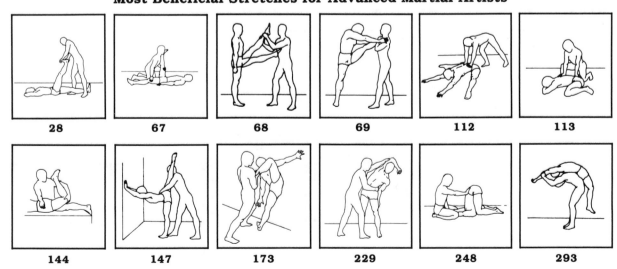

28   67   68   69   112   113

144   147   173   229   248   293

SKIING

<table>
<tr><th colspan="6">Stretching Routine for Skiing</th></tr>
<tr>
<th>Body
part</th><th>Stretch
number</th>
<th>Body
part</th><th>Stretch
number</th>
<th>Body
part</th><th>Stretch
number</th>
</tr>
<tr>
<td>Plantar arch</td><td>4</td>
<td>Hip flexors</td><td>135-137,
144-145</td>
<td>Chest/
pectoralis</td><td>254, 257,
261</td>
</tr>
<tr>
<td>Anterior toes</td><td>5</td>
<td>Buttocks
& hips</td><td>152-153, 156,
159, 162, 165,
166, **170, 172**</td>
<td>Anterior
shoulder</td><td>264-266,
268-270</td>
</tr>
<tr>
<td>Ankles/Anterior
lower leg</td><td>7, 11</td>
<td>Abdomen
& hips</td><td>178-179,
195</td>
<td>Lateral
shoulder</td><td>271</td>
</tr>
<tr>
<td>Ankles/Lateral
lower leg</td><td>13, 19, 22</td>
<td>Lower
back</td><td>198, 200, **201**,
202, 205, 207</td>
<td>Internal
rotators</td><td>273, **277**</td>
</tr>
<tr>
<td>Achilles tendon</td><td>25, **28***, 30,
32</td>
<td>Lateral
trunk</td><td>221-222, **229**</td>
<td>External
rotators</td><td>**282**, 284-
285</td>
</tr>
<tr>
<td>Back of knee</td><td>45</td>
<td>Upper
back</td><td>234</td>
<td>Shoulder
flexors</td><td>286-287,
**289, 291,
293**</td>
</tr>
<tr>
<td>Hamstrings</td><td>53, 55, 58,
67</td>
<td>Posterior
neck</td><td>237, 242,
247</td>
<td>Biceps</td><td>296</td>
</tr>
<tr>
<td>Adductors</td><td>87, 96,
105</td>
<td>Lateral
neck</td><td>250</td>
<td>Triceps</td><td>299, 301,
303</td>
</tr>
<tr>
<td>Quadriceps</td><td>123-124,
129</td>
<td>Anterior
neck</td><td>252</td>
<td>Wrist
extensors</td><td>305-306</td>
</tr>
<tr>
<td></td><td></td>
<td></td><td></td>
<td>Wrist
flexors</td><td>308-310</td>
</tr>
<tr><td colspan="6">*Boldfaced numbers indicate partner stretches.</td></tr>
</table>

Most Beneficial Stretches for Skiers

22   30   45   58   87   124

153   156   165   179   202   264

SOCCER

Stretching Routine for Soccer					
Body part	*Stretch number*	*Body part*	*Stretch number*	*Body part*	*Stretch number*
Plantar arch	3, 4	Hip flexors	135-137, **144-145**	Chest/ pectoralis	254, 257, **261**
Anterior toes	6	Buttocks & hips	152-154, 159, 162, 165, **170, 172**	Anterior shoulder	264-265, **268-270**
Ankles/Anterior lower leg	7, 11	Abdomen & hips	178, 179, **195**	Lateral shoulder	271
Ankles/Lateral lower leg	13, 15, 19-20	Lower back	198, 200, **201**, 205, 207	Internal rotators	273, **277**
Achilles tendon	23, 25, **28***, 30, 32	Lateral trunk	221-222, **229**	External rotators	**282**, 284-285
Back of knee	45	Upper back	234	Shoulder flexors	286, **291, 293**
Hamstrings	53, 55, **67**	Posterior neck	237, 242, **247**	Biceps	296
Adductors	87, 89, 91, 96, **105**	Lateral neck	250	Triceps	299, 301, **303**
Quadriceps	123, **129**	Anterior neck	252	Wrist extensors	305-306
				Wrist flexors	308-310

*Boldfaced numbers indicate partner stretches.

Most Beneficial Stretches for Soccer Players

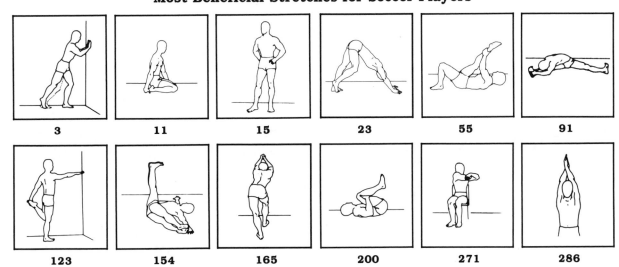

3   11   15   23   55   91

123   154   165   200   271   286

SWIMMING

Stretching Routine for Swimming					
Body part	*Stretch number*	*Body part*	*Stretch number*	*Body part*	*Stretch number*
Plantar arch	4	Hip flexors	135-137, **144-145**	Chest/ pectoralis	254, 257, 260, **261**
Anterior toes	5-6	Buttocks & hips	152-153, 159, 162, **170, 172**	Anterior shoulder	264-265, **268-270**
Ankles/Anterior lower leg	7, 11	Abdomen & hips	178-179, **195**	Lateral shoulder	271
Ankles/Lateral lower leg	13, 19	Lower back	198, 200, **201**, 205, 207	Internal rotators	273, **277**
Achilles tendon	25, **28***, 30, 32	Lateral trunk	221-222, **229**	External rotators	**282**, 284-285
Back of knee	45	Upper back	234	Shoulder flexors	286, **291-293**
Hamstrings	53, 55, **67**	Posterior neck	237, 242, **247**	Biceps	296
Adductors	87, 89, 96, **105**	Lateral neck	250	Triceps	299, 301, **303**
Quadriceps	123, 125, **129**	Anterior neck	252	Wrist extensors	305-306
				Wrist flexors	308-310
*Boldfaced numbers indicate partner stretches.					

Most Beneficial Stretches for Swimmers

234　　　260　　　265　　　269　　　271　　　277

284　　　286　　　291　　　293　　　299　　　301

TENNIS

Stretching Routine for Tennis					
Body part	*Stretch number*	*Body part*	*Stretch number*	*Body part*	*Stretch number*
Plantar arch	3-4	Hip flexors	135-137, **144-145**	Chest/ pectoralis	254, 257, **261**
Anterior toes	6	Buttocks & hips	149, 152-153, 159, 162, **170, 172**	Anterior shoulder	264-265, **268-270**
Ankles/Anterior lower leg	7, 11	Abdomen & hips	178-179, **195**	Lateral shoulder	271
Ankles/Lateral lower leg	13, 16, 19-20	Lower back	198, 200, **201**, 205, 207	Internal rotators	273, **277**
Achilles tendon	21, 25, 27, **28***, 30, 32	Lateral trunk	221-222, **229**	External rotators	**282**, 284-285
Back of knee	45-46	Upper back	234	Shoulder flexors	286, **291**
Hamstrings	53, 55, 57, **67**	Posterior neck	237, 242, **247**	Biceps	296
Adductors	87, 92, 96, **105**	Lateral neck	250	Triceps	299, 301, **303**
Quadriceps	123, **129**	Anterior neck	252	Wrist extensors	305-306
				Wrist flexors	308-310
*Boldfaced numbers indicate partner stretches.					

Most Beneficial Stretches for Tennis Players

3   11   21   30   57   92

123   149   221   265   277   306

TRACK AND FIELD

Stretching Routine for Track and Field—High Jump (Fosbury Flop)					
Body part	*Stretch number*	*Body part*	*Stretch number*	*Body part*	*Stretch number*
Plantar arch	3, 4	Hip flexors	135-137, **144-145**	Chest/ pectoralis	254, 257, **261**
Anterior toes	6	Buttocks & hips	152-153, 159, 162	Anterior shoulder	264-265, **268-270**
Ankles/Anterior lower leg	7, 11	Abdomen & hips	176, 178-179, 181, 188-190, **195-196**	Lateral shoulder	271
Ankles/Lateral lower leg	13, 19	Lower back	185, 198, 200, **201**, 205, 207	Internal rotators	273, **277**
Achilles tendon	23, 25, **28***, 30, 32	Lateral trunk	221-222, **229**	External rotators	**282**, 284-285
Back of knee	45-46	Upper back	234	Shoulder flexors	286, **291**
Hamstrings	53, 55, **67**	Posterior neck	237, 242, **247**	Biceps	296
Adductors	87, 96, **116**	Lateral neck	250	Triceps	299, 301, **303**
Quadriceps	123, 124, **129**	Anterior neck	252	Wrist extensors	305-306
				Wrist flexors	308-310
*Boldfaced numbers indicate partner stretches.					

Most Beneficial Stretches for High Jumpers (Fosbury Flop)

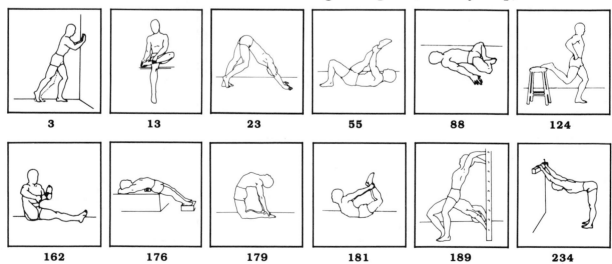

3　　13　　23　　55　　88　　124

162　　176　　179　　181　　189　　234

TRACK AND FIELD

Stretching Routine for Track and Field—High Jump (Straddle)					
Body part	*Stretch number*	*Body part*	*Stretch number*	*Body part*	*Stretch number*
Plantar arch	3, 4	Hip flexors	135-137, **144-145**	Chest/ pectoralis	254, 257, **261**
Anterior toes	6	Buttocks & hips	149, 152-153, 159, 161-162	Anterior shoulder	264-265, **268-270**
Ankles/Anterior lower leg	7, 11	Abdomen & hips	178-179, **195-196**	Lateral shoulder	271
Ankles/Lateral lower leg	13, 19	Lower back	198, 200, **201**, 205, 207	Internal rotators	273, **277**
Achilles tendon	25, **28***, 30, 32	Lateral trunk	220-222, **229**	External rotators	**282**, 284-285
Back of knee	45-46	Upper back	234	Shoulder flexors	286, **291**
Hamstrings	53, 55, 57-58, **67**	Posterior neck	237, 242, **247**	Biceps	296
Adductors	87, 90-91, 96, 98-100, **116**	Lateral neck	250	Triceps	299, 301, **303**
Quadriceps	123, **129**	Anterior neck	252	Wrist extensors	305-306
				Wrist flexors	308-310

*Boldfaced numbers indicate partner stretches.

Most Beneficial Stretches for High Jumpers (Straddle)

3   13   25   57   58   91

98   99   149   161   220   221

TRACK AND FIELD

Stretching Routine for Track and Field—Hurdles & Sprints					
Body part	*Stretch number*	*Body part*	*Stretch number*	*Body part*	*Stretch number*
Plantar arch	4	Hip flexors	135-137, **144-145**	Chest/ pectoralis	254, 257, **261**
Anterior toes	6	Buttocks & hips	149, 151-153, 159, 162	Anterior shoulder	264-265, **268-270**
Ankles/Anterior lower leg	7, 11	Abdomen & hips	178-179, **195-196**	Lateral shoulder	271
Ankles/Lateral lower leg	13, 16, 19-20	Lower back	198, 200, **201**, 204-205, 207	Internal rotators	273, **277**
Achilles tendon	25-26, **28***, 30, 32	Lateral trunk	221-222, **229**	External rotators	**282**, 284-285
Back of knee	45-46	Upper back	234	Shoulder flexors	286, **291**
Hamstrings	53, 55, 58, **67-68**	Posterior neck	237, 242, **247**	Biceps	296
Adductors	87, 96, 98, 101, **105, 115-116**	Lateral neck	250	Triceps	299, 301, **303**
Quadriceps	123-124, 127, **129**	Anterior neck	252	Wrist extensors	305-306
				Wrist flexors	308-310

*Boldfaced numbers indicate partner stretches.

Most Beneficial Stretches for Hurdlers and Sprinters

4   11   32   58   98   115

124   127   136   149   151   204

TRACK AND FIELD

Stretching Routine for Track and Field—Javelin & Discus					
Body part	*Stretch number*	*Body part*	*Stretch number*	*Body part*	*Stretch number*
Plantar arch	4	Hip flexors	135-137, **144-145**	Chest/ pectoralis	254, 257, **261**
Anterior toes	5	Buttocks & hips	152-153, 159, 162	Anterior shoulder	264-265, **268-270**
Ankles/Anterior lower leg	7, 11	Abdomen & hips	178-179, **195-196**	Lateral shoulder	271
Ankles/Lateral lower leg	13, 19	Lower back	198, 200, **201**, 205, 207	Internal rotators	273, **277**
Achilles tendon	21, 25, **28***, 30, 32	Lateral trunk	221-222, **229**, 230, 232	External rotators	**282** 284-285
Back of knee	45	Upper back	234	Shoulder flexors	286, **291**
Hamstrings	53, 55, **67**	Posterior neck	237, 242, **247**	Biceps	296
Adductors	87, 96, **105**	Lateral neck	250	Triceps	299, 301, **303**
Quadriceps	121, 123, **129**	Anterior neck	252	Wrist extensors	305-306
				Wrist flexors	308-310
*Boldfaced numbers indicate partner stretches.					

Most Beneficial Stretches for Javelin and Discus Throwers

5	21	55	87	123	137

159	179	230	265	271	299

VOLLEYBALL

Stretching Routine for Volleyball					
Body part	*Stretch number*	*Body part*	*Stretch number*	*Body part*	*Stretch number*
Plantar arch	2, 4	Hip flexors	135-137, **144-145**	Chest/ pectoralis	254, 257, **261**
Anterior toes	6	Buttocks & hips	152-153, 159, 161-162, **170, 172**	Anterior shoulder	264-265, **268-270**
Ankles/Anterior lower leg	7, 11	Abdomen & hips	178-179, **195**	Lateral shoulder	271
Ankles/Lateral lower leg	13, 17, 19-20	Lower back	198, 200, **201**, 205, 207	Internal rotators	273, **277**
Achilles tendon	25, **28***, 30, 32	Lateral trunk	219, 221-222, **229**	External rotators	**282**, 284-285
Back of knee	45	Upper back	234	Shoulder flexors	286, **291**
Hamstrings	53, 55, **67**	Posterior neck	237, 242, **247**	Biceps	296
Adductors	87, 91, 96, **105**	Lateral neck	250	Triceps	299, 301, **303**
Quadriceps	123, 127, **129**	Anterior neck	252	Wrist extensors	305-306
				Wrist flexors	308-310
*Boldfaced numbers indicate partner stretches.					

Most Beneficial Stretches for Volleyball Players

4   13   25   55   91   127

152   161   178   219   264   301

WEIGHT LIFTING

Stretching Routine for Weight Lifting					
Body part	*Stretch number*	*Body part*	*Stretch number*	*Body part*	*Stretch number*
Plantar arch	4	Hip flexors	135-137, **144-145**	Chest/pectoralis	254, 257, **261**
Anterior toes	5	Buttocks & hips	149, 152-153, 156, 159, 162, **170, 172**	Anterior shoulder	264-265, **268-270**
Ankles/Anterior lower leg	7, 11	Abdomen & hips	178-179, **195**	Lateral shoulder	271
Ankles/Lateral lower leg	13, 19	Lower back	198, 200, **201**, 205, 207	Internal rotators	273, **277**
Achilles tendon	25, **28***, 30-32, 36-37	Lateral trunk	219, 221-222, **229**, 232	External rotators	**282**, 284-285
Back of knee	45	Upper back	234	Shoulder flexors	286, **291**
Hamstrings	53, 55, **67**	Posterior neck	237, 242, **247**	Biceps	296
Adductors	87, 91, 96, **105**, 119	Lateral neck	250	Triceps	299, 301, **303**
Quadriceps	123, 125-126, **129**	Anterior neck	252	Wrist extensors	305-306
				Wrist flexors	308-310

*Boldfaced numbers indicate partner stretches.

Most Beneficial Stretches for Weight Lifters

36	53	91	126	149	156

198	200	222	234	265	296

WEIGHT LIFTING

Stretching Routine for Weight Lifting With Very Light Weights					
Body part	*Stretch number*	*Body part*	*Stretch number*	*Body part*	*Stretch number*
Plantar arch	—	Hip flexors	118-119	Chest/ pectoralis	262
Anterior toes	—	Buttocks & hips	118-119	Anterior shoulder	—
Ankles/Anterior lower leg	—	Abdomen & hips	—	Lateral shoulder	—
Ankles/Lateral lower leg	—	Lower back	84-85	Internal rotators	278
Achilles tendon	42-43	Lateral trunk	230-232	External rotators	—
Back of knee	—	Upper back	—	Shoulder flexors	294
Hamstrings	84-85	Posterior neck	—	Biceps	297
Adductors	118-119	Lateral neck	—	Triceps	304
Quadriceps	120, 131	Anterior neck	—	Wrist extensors	—
				Wrist flexors	—

Most Beneficial Stretches for Weight Lifters Using Very Light Weights

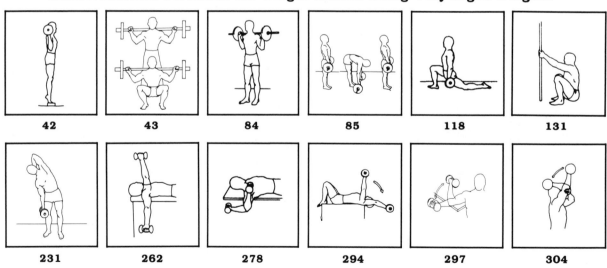

42   43   84   85   118   131

231   262   278   294   297   304

WRESTLING

Stretching Routine for Wrestling					
Body part	*Stretch number*	*Body part*	*Stretch number*	*Body part*	*Stretch number*
Plantar arch	2, 4	Hip flexors	135-137, **144-145**	Chest/ pectoralis	254, 257, **261**
Anterior toes	6	Buttocks & hips	152-153, 156, 159, 162, **170, 172**	Anterior shoulder	264-265, **268-270**
Ankles/Anterior lower leg	7, 11	Abdomen & hips	178-179, 186-187, **195**	Lateral shoulder	271
Ankles/Lateral lower leg	13, 19	Lower back	198, 200, **201**, 205, 207	Internal rotators	273, **277**
Achilles tendon	23, 25, **28***, 30, 32	Lateral trunk	221-222, **229**	External rotators	**282**, 284-285
Back of knee	45	Upper back	234	Shoulder flexors	286, 287, **291**
Hamstrings	53, 55, **67**	Posterior neck	239, 244-246, **247**	Biceps	296
Adductors	87, 91, 96, **105**, 114	Lateral neck	250	Triceps	299, 301, **303**
Quadriceps	123, **129**, 134	Anterior neck	252-253	Wrist extensors	305-306
				Wrist flexors	308-310
*Boldfaced numbers indicate partner stretches.					

Most Beneficial Stretches for Wrestlers

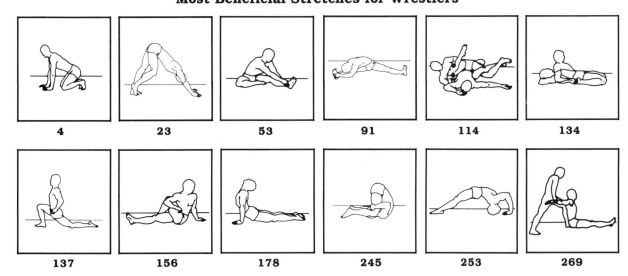

4   23   53   91   114   134

137   156   178   245   253   269

ACTIVE PERSON

Stretching Routine for the Active Person					
Body part	*Stretch number*	*Body part*	*Stretch number*	*Body part*	*Stretch number*
Plantar arch	4	Hip flexors	137	Chest/pectoralis	255, 259
Anterior toes	5	Buttocks & hips	153, 155, 163-164	Anterior shoulder	263-264
Ankles/Anterior lower leg	7	Abdomen & hips	178	Lateral shoulder	270
Ankles/Lateral lower leg	13	Lower back	197-198, 200, 208	Internal rotators	273, 275
Achilles tendon	25, 30, 32, 35	Lateral trunk	216-217	External rotators	279
Back of knee	44-45, 49	Upper back	233-234	Shoulder flexors	286
Hamstrings	53-54, 56, 72	Posterior neck	237-238	Biceps	295-296
Adductors	86-87	Lateral neck	250	Triceps	298-299
Quadriceps	123	Anterior neck	251-252	Wrist extensors	305
				Wrist flexors	308, 311

Most Beneficial Stretches for Active People

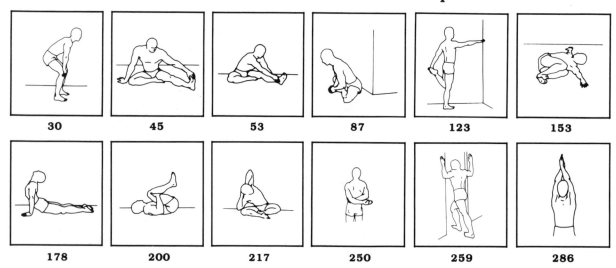

30   45   53   87   123   153

178   200   217   250   259   286

OLDER ATHLETE

Stretching Routine for the Older Athlete					
Body part	*Stretch number*	*Body part*	*Stretch number*	*Body part*	*Stretch number*
Plantar arch	1	Hip flexors	100	Chest/ pectoralis	256, 258
Anterior toes	5	Buttocks & hips	148, 155	Anterior shoulder	264
Ankles/Anterior lower leg	7	Abdomen & hips	177	Lateral shoulder	271
Ankles/Lateral lower leg	13-14	Lower back	198-199	Internal rotators	273
Achilles tendon	21, 29-30	Lateral trunk	216-217	External rotators	279
Back of knee	44, 49	Upper back	233	Shoulder flexors	286
Hamstrings	53-54	Posterior neck	237-238	Biceps	295-296
Adductors	86-87, 91	Lateral neck	249	Triceps	299
Quadriceps	121-122	Anterior neck	252	Wrist extensors	305
				Wrist flexors	308

Most Beneficial Stretches for the Older Athlete

■ To eliminate risk of injury, perform all stretches from a sitting or lying position for maximum balance and support.

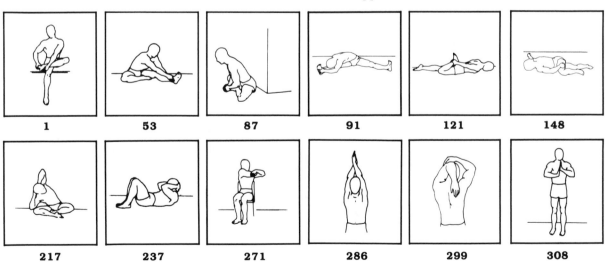

1 53 87 91 121 148

217 237 271 286 299 308

ILLUSTRATED INSTRUCTIONS FOR 311 STRETCHES

Before starting any exercise program, you should have a medical examination. You should also be examined at regular intervals throughout the program, or at any time irregular conditions such as dizziness, pain in the chest, or other symptoms appear.

The stretches that follow are arranged in a systematic order by the muscle group or joints to be stretched and by their relative difficulty or risk of injury. As a general rule, this was determined by the height of the athlete's center of gravity, the use of a partner, and the use of weights or other mechanical aids.

Several of the following stretches are potentially dangerous for the average person and for the advanced athlete recovering from an injury. Furthermore, special care *must* be exercised for those stretches in which the direction of the force is accentuated by a partner. At no time should you compromise your joints' integrity. These advanced stretches are incorporated specifically for individuals involved in such disciplines as dance, gymnastics, the martial arts, wrestling, and yoga, and they are marked with a "caution" sign. If you lack adequate expertise and knowledge, you should seek out a certified and experienced instructor or trainer.

The stretches that follow should be executed in a slow or static manner. However, if you are more advanced and under proper supervision, you may find it more effective and efficient to incorporate the contract-relax PNF strategy. Descriptions of this technique can be read on page 10. Also review the prestretching and stretching guidelines on page 18.

Finally, the instructions for the following stretches are written for one side of the body only. Where appropriate, repeat the stretch on the other side.

Key to Symbols

 = This stretch should be avoided by those with a bad back.

 = This stretch should be avoided by those with bad knees.

 = This stretch should be avoided by those with hyperextended knees.

 = This stretch should be avoided by those with a bad neck.

 = Caution: This stretch is potentially dangerous for the average person and for the advanced athlete recovering from an injury. This exercise is for advanced athletes in good health only.

FEET

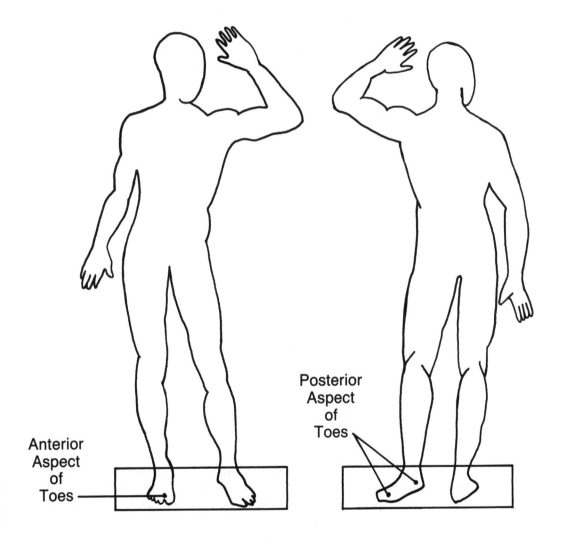

Anterior
Aspect
of
Toes

Posterior
Aspect
of
Toes

Plantar Arch

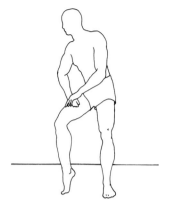

Stretch # 1

1. Sit upright in a chair or on the floor with one leg crossed over the opposite knee.
2. Grasp hold of your ankle with one hand.
3. Grasp hold of the underside of your toes and ball of the foot.
4. Exhale, and pull your toes backward (extension of the toes).
5. Hold the stretch and relax.

Stretch # 2

1. Stand upright with one leg slightly in front of the other.
2. Exhale, shift your weight onto the ball of your forward foot, and press downward.
3. Hold the stretch and relax.

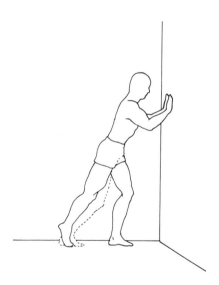

Stretch # 3

1. Stand upright 2 or 3 steps from a wall.
2. Bend one leg forward and keep the opposite leg straight.
3. Lean slightly against the wall.
4. Keep your rear foot down, flat, and parallel to your hips.
5. Exhale, raise the rear heel off the floor shifting your weight onto the ball of your rear foot, and press downward.
6. Hold the stretch and relax.

Stretch # 4 (Both Feet)

1. Kneel on all fours with your toes underneath you.
2. Exhale, and lower your buttocks backward and downward.
3. Hold the stretch and relax.

Anterior Aspect of the Toes

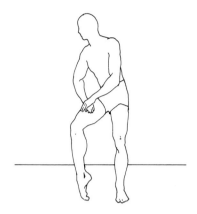

Stretch # 5

1. Sit upright in a chair or on the floor with one leg crossed over the opposite knee.
2. Grasp hold of your ankle and the heel of your foot with one hand.
3. Grasp hold of the top portion of your foot and toes with your other hand.
4. Exhale, and slowly pull the back of your toes to the ball of your foot (flexion).
5. Hold the stretch and relax.

Stretch # 6

1. Stand upright with one leg slightly in front of the other.
2. Turn your forward foot under so the top portion of your toes contacts the floor.
3. Exhale, shift your weight forward, and press your toes downward.
4. Hold the stretch and relax.

LOWER LEGS
AND KNEES

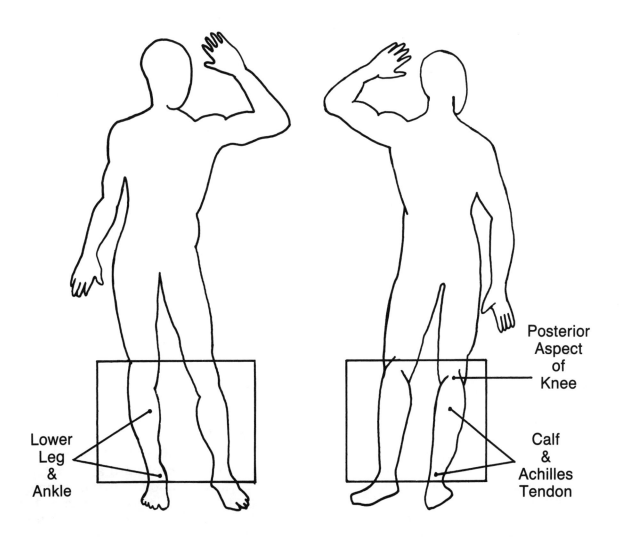

Lower
Leg
&
Ankle

Posterior
Aspect
of
Knee

Calf
&
Achilles
Tendon

Ankles and Anterior Lower Leg

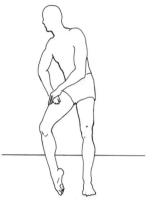

Stretch # 7

1. Sit upright in a chair or on the floor with one leg crossed over the opposite knee.
2. Grasp hold on or above your ankle or heel of your foot with one hand.
3. Grasp hold of the top portion of your foot with your other hand.
4. Exhale, and slowly pull the bottom of your foot to your body (plantar flexion).
5. Hold the stretch and relax.

Stretch # 8

1. Stand upright with one leg slightly in front of the other.
2. Turn your forward foot under so the top portion rests on the floor.
3. Exhale, shift your weight forward, and extend (increase the angle of) the ankle joint.
4. Hold the stretch and relax.

Stretch # 9

1. Kneel on all fours with your toes pointing backward. If this is uncomfortable, place a blanket under your shins.
2. Exhale, and slowly sit on your heels (if you can).
3. Hold the stretch and relax.

Stretch # 10

1. Kneel upright on the floor with your toes facing backward and your feet elevated by a folded mat or cushion.
2. Exhale, and slowly lower your buttocks onto your heels (if you can).
3. Hold the stretch and relax.

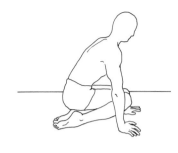

Stretch # 11

1. Kneel on all fours with your toes pointing backward. If this is uncomfortable, place a blanket under your shins.
2. Exhale, and slowly sit on your heels (if you can).
3. Reach around, grasp the top portion of your toes, and pull them toward your head.
4. Hold the stretch and relax.
■ This stretch is used to prevent "shin-splints."

Stretch # 12

1. Kneel on all fours with your toes facing backward.
2. Exhale, and slowly sit on your heels.
3. Inhale, and shift your weight backward so that your knees lift slightly off the floor. Use your hands for support to adjust the proper weight onto the ankle joints.
4. Hold the stretch and relax.

Ankles and Lateral Lower Leg

Stretch # 13 (One Leg)

1. Sit upright in a chair or on the floor with one leg crossed over the opposite knee.
2. Grasp your ankle and the heel of your foot with one hand.
3. Grasp the top outside portion of your foot with the other hand.
4. Exhale, and slowly invert your ankle (turn it inward).
5. Hold the stretch and relax.

Stretch # 14 (One Leg)

1. Sit upright on the floor with both legs straight.
2. Keep one leg straight and position your opposite leg so its heel touches the groin of your extended leg.
3. Exhale, bend forward at the waist, and grasp your foot. Wrap a folded towel around your foot and grasp the ends of it if you are unable to reach your foot.
4. Exhale, and slowly invert your ankle (turn it inward).
5. Hold the stretch and relax.

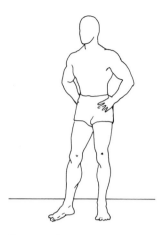

Stretch # 15 (One Leg)

1. Stand upright with one or both hands on your hips. If necessary, use a wall for balance and support.
2. Turn one foot under so that the top outside portion rests on the floor.
3. Exhale, slowly invert your ankle, and press your foot downward.
4. Hold the stretch and relax.

Stretch # 16

1. Sit upright on the floor with both legs straight and straddled.
2. Exhale, bend forward at the waist, and grasp both feet. Wrap two folded towels around your feet and grasp the ends of them if you cannot reach your feet.
3. Exhale, and slowly invert both ankles (turn them inward).
4. Hold the stretch and relax.

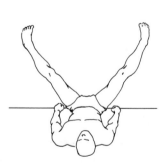

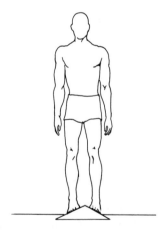

Stretch # 17

1. Lie flat on your back with both legs raised and your buttocks against a wall.
2. Straddle both legs.
3. Exhale, and slowly invert both ankles (turn them inward).
4. Hold the stretch and relax.

Stretch # 18

1. Stand upright on an incline board cut at a 45-degree angle.
2. Hold the stretch and relax.

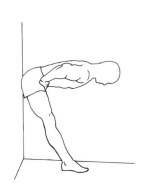

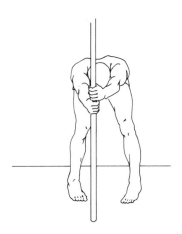

Stretch # 19

1. Stand upright with your back and heels flat against a wall.
2. Slide your feet 1 to 2 feet away from the wall, turn your feet inward, and invert the ankles.
3. Exhale, and slowly flex forward.
4. Hold the stretch and relax.

 If you have a "bad back," round your upper torso rather than lifting up with an arched back.

Stretch # 20

1. Stand upright with both hands grasping a pillar for support.
2. Straddle your feet hip-width, ankles inverted and feet toed-in, approximately 1 or 2 feet from the pillar.
3. Exhale, flex at the waist, and shift your hips backward to form a 45-degree angle with your legs.
4. Hold the stretch and relax.
5. Exhale, use the pillar for support, and bend the knees when returning to an upright position.

Achilles Tendon and Posterior Lower Leg

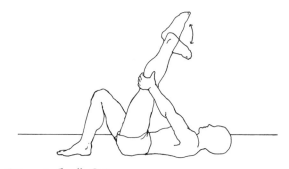

Stretch # 21

1. Lie on your back with legs extended.
2. Flex one leg and slide the foot toward the buttocks.
3. Raise the opposite leg toward your face and grasp behind the knee.
4. Exhale, and slowly flex the foot toward your face.
5. Hold the stretch and relax.

 If you have a "bad back," flex the extended leg and slowly lower it to the floor.

Stretch # 22

1. Assume a kneeling position.
2. Inhale, and shift one foot slightly forward, placing it flat on the floor.
3. Exhale, and lean forward.
4. Hold the stretch and relax.

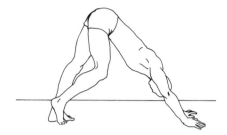

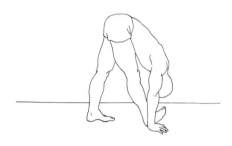

Stretch # 23

1. Assume a front prone support (push-up) position.
2. Move your hands closer to your feet to raise your hips and form a triangle. This position can also be modified by resting your elbows and/or head on the floor.
3. At the highest point of the triangle, slowly press your heels to the floor, or in an alternating manner flex one knee while keeping your opposite leg extended.

 The latter method is commonly employed in a ballistic or rhythmic manner that could result in soreness.

Stretch # 24

1. Assume a kneeling position.
2. Inhale, and shift one foot slightly forward, placing it flat on the floor.
3. Inhale, and slowly extend your legs.
4. Exhale, lower your head to the forward foot, and flex the ankle.
5. Hold the stretch and relax.

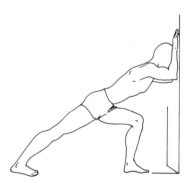

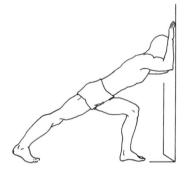

Stretch # 25

1. Stand upright 4 or 5 steps from a wall.
2. Bend one leg forward and keep your opposite leg straight.
3. Lean against the wall without losing the straight line of your head, neck, spine, pelvis, outstretched leg, and ankle.
4. Keep your rear foot down, flat, and parallel to your hips.
5. Exhale, bend your arms, move your chest toward the wall, and shift your weight forward.
6. Hold the stretch and relax.

Stretch # 26

1. Stand upright 4 or 5 steps from a wall.
2. Bend one leg forward and keep your opposite leg straight.
3. Lean against the wall without losing the straight line of your head, neck, spine, pelvis, outstretched leg, and ankle.
4. Keep your rear heel raised and parallel to your hips.
5. Exhale, bend your arms, move your chest toward the wall, and shift your weight forward.
6. Exhale, and slowly attempt to press your rear heel to the floor.
7. Hold the stretch and relax.

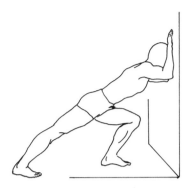

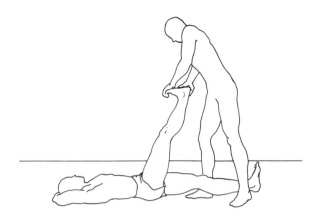

Stretch # 27

1. Stand upright 4 or 5 steps from a wall.
2. Bend one leg forward and keep your opposite leg straight.
3. Lean against the wall without losing the straight line of your head, neck, spine, pelvis, right leg and ankle.
4. Keep your rear foot down, flat, and parallel to your hips.
5. Exhale, and flex your forward knee toward the floor.
6. Hold the stretch and relax.

Stretch # 28

1. Lie flat on your back with one leg raised.
2. Your partner straddles your lower leg, with one hand grasping the heel of the raised foot and the opposite hand placed underneath the toes and ball of the foot.
3. Exhale as you passively allow your partner to flex the foot while keeping the leg extended.
4. Hold the stretch and relax.

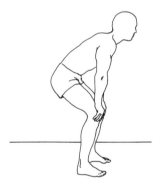

Stretch # 29

1. Place an incline board facing a wall.
2. Stand upright on the incline board with your hands flat against the wall, and lean forward.
3. Hold the stretch and relax.

Stretch # 30

1. Stand upright with both hands on your hips or knees. If necessary, hold onto a wall for balance.
2. Keep your heels down, flat, and parallel.
3. Exhale, and slowly flex your knees, bringing them as close to the floor as possible.
4. Hold the stretch and relax.

Stretch # 31

1. Stand upright with the balls of your feet balanced on an edge or step.
2. Exhale, and slowly lower your heels to the floor.
3. Hold the stretch and relax.

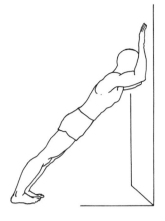

Stretch # 32

1. Stand upright 4 or 5 steps from a wall.
2. Lean against the wall without losing the straight line of the head, neck, spine, pelvis, legs, and ankles.
3. Keep both heels down, flat, together, and parallel to the hips.
4. Exhale, bend your arms, move your chest toward the wall, and shift your weight forward.
5. Hold the stretch and relax.

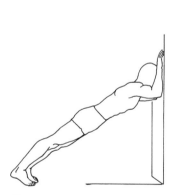

Stretch # 33

1. Stand upright 4 or 5 steps from a wall.
2. Lean against the wall without losing the straight line of the head, neck, spine, pelvis, legs, and ankles.
3. Keep both of the heels raised, together, and parallel to your hips.
4. Exhale, bend your arms, move your chest toward the wall, and shift your weight forward.
5. Exhale, and slowly attempt to press your heels to the floor.
6. Hold the stretch and relax.

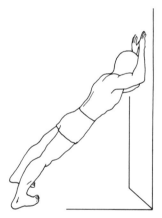

Stretch # 34

1. Stand upright 4 or 5 steps from a wall.
2. Lean against the wall without losing the straight line of the head, neck, spine, pelvis, legs, and ankles.
3. Keep both of the feet down, flat, and toed-in shoulder-width apart.
4. Exhale, bend your arms, move your chest toward the wall, and shift your weight forward.
5. Hold the stretch and relax.

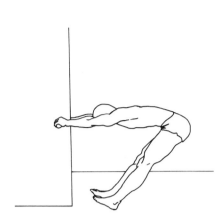

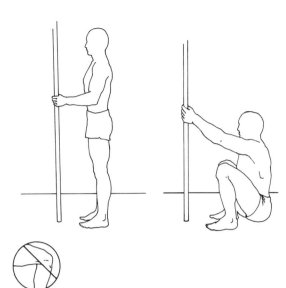

Stretch # 35

1. Stand upright approximately 2 feet from an open door.
2. Grasp the door handles with both hands.
3. Lift the front part of your feet and balance on your heels.
4. Exhale, keep both legs straight, and shift your hips backward.
5. Hold the stretch and relax.

▼ Those with "bad backs" should bend the knees when returning to an upright position.

Stretch # 36

1. Stand upright holding a pole and with your feet parallel about 1 foot apart.
2. Inhale, and lower your buttocks to the floor, keeping the back straight and the heels flat on the floor.
3. Hold the stretch and relax.
4. Exhale, and return to the starting position.

■ The following five exercises use the body positions I—V traditionally used in dance. During the execution of these exercises it is imperative to avoid initiating the "turnout" from the knees. This action must come from the hips and be controlled by the interaction between the external rotators and internal rotators of the hip joint. In addition, you must concentrate on keeping your weight distributed equally as your heels are maintained flat on the floor. Failure to use proper technique can result in injury to your knees, legs, or feet!

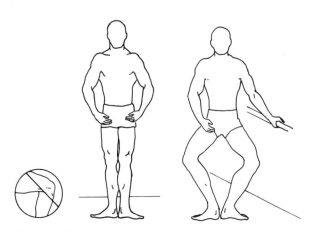

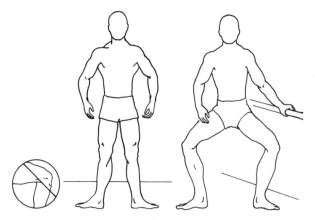

Stretch # 37

1. Stand upright, feet together, hands on hips.
2. Turn to Position I with your heels together and your toes pointing outward at a 90-degree angle.
3. Grasp a surface for support and balance.
4. Exhale, and slowly flex your knees, initiating the turnout from your hips.
5. Hold the stretch and relax.

Stretch # 38

1. Stand upright, feet together, hands on your hips.
2. Turn to Position II with your heels about 12 inches apart, toes pointing outward at a 90-degree angle, and feet in line with each other.
3. Grasp a surface for support and balance.
4. Exhale, and slowly flex your knees, initiating the turnout from your hips.
5. Hold the stretch and relax.

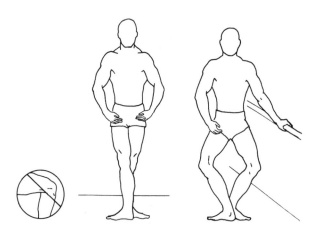

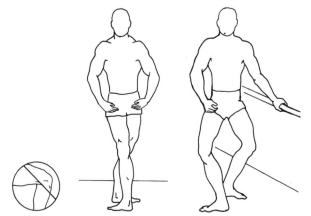

Stretch # 39

1. Stand upright, feet together, hands on your hips.
2. Turn to Position III so your feet are in line, pressed together, the heel of one foot at the arch or instep of the other foot, and the toes pointing away (in opposite directions from each other).
3. Grasp a surface for support and balance.
4. Exhale, and slowly flex your knees, initiating the turnout from your hips.
5. Hold the stretch and relax.

Stretch # 40

1. Stand upright, feet together, hands on your hips.
2. Turn to Position IV with one foot approximately 12 inches in front of the other, the heel of your forward foot in line with the toes of your back foot, and your feet pointed in the opposite direction.
3. Grasp a surface for support and balance.
4. Exhale, and slowly flex your knees, initiating the turnout from your hips.
5. Hold the stretch and relax.

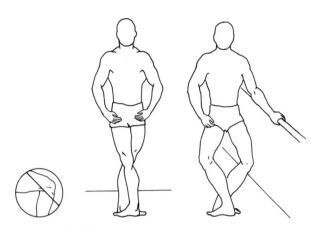

Stretch # 41

1. Stand upright, feet together, hands on your hips.
2. Turn to Position V with the heel of your front foot flat against the toe of your other foot; at the same time, the heel of your rear foot is against the toe of your front foot, and your feet are pointed in opposite directions.
3. Grasp a surface for support and balance.
4. Exhale, and slowly flex your knees, initiating the turnout from your hips.
5. Hold the stretch and relax.

Stretch # 42

1. Stand upright with toes and balls of your feet on a thick board and with a light barbell resting across your shoulders.
2. Exhale, and rise up on your toes as high as possible.
3. Inhale, and lower your heels until they almost touch the floor.
4. Hold the stretch and relax.

Stretch # 43

1. Stand upright with your feet about shoulder-width apart and with a light barbell resting on your shoulders.
2. Inhale, and slowly lower your buttocks toward the floor while keeping the heels flat on the floor.
3. Hold the stretch at the bottom.
4. Exhale, and return to the starting position.

 This stretch is very controversial. Always use a light weight that can be handled easily. Furthermore, the use of a lifting belt is strongly recommended to provide extra support.

Back of the Knees

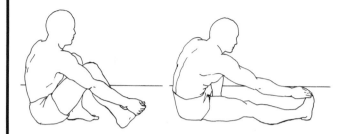

Stretch # 44 (One Leg)

1. Sit upright on the floor, knees flexed and grasping the toes of one foot.
2. Exhale, and slowly extend the leg.
3. Exhale, and pull back on the foot.
4. Hold the stretch and relax.

Stretch # 45 (One Leg)

1. Sit upright with the legs straight.
2. Keep one leg straight, and position the opposite leg so its heel touches the groin of your extended leg.
3. Exhale, lean forward, and grasp your foot.
4. Exhale, keep your leg straight, and pull on your foot.
5. Hold the stretch and relax.

Stretch # 46 (One Leg)

1. Sit upright on the floor with both legs straight.
2. Cross one leg and rest it on the opposing knee.
3. Exhale, lean forward, and grasp your foot. If you can't reach your foot, fold a blanket or towel and wrap it around your foot, holding on to both ends.
4. Exhale, keep your leg straight, and pull on your foot.
5. Hold the stretch and relax.

Stretch # 47 (One Leg)

1. Stand upright 4 or 5 steps from a wall.
2. Bend one leg forward and keep your opposite leg straight.
3. Lean against the wall without losing the straight line of your head, neck, spine, pelvis, rear leg, and ankle.
4. Keep your rear foot down, flat, and parallel to your hips.
5. Exhale, bend your arms, move your chest toward the wall, and shift your weight forward.
6. Exhale, and slowly contract the quadriceps of your rear leg without excessively jamming or locking the knee.
7. Hold the stretch and relax.

Stretch # 48 (One Leg)

1. Stand upright on the floor with one leg crossed over the other.
2. Exhale, keeping one leg straight, extend your upper back, bend forward at the waist, and lower your trunk onto your thigh.
3. Hold the stretch and relax.
4. Exhale, bend the knees or round the upper torso up rather than lifting with an arched back when returning to an upright position.

Stretch # 49

1. Sit upright on the floor with both legs straight.
2. Exhale, lean forward, and grasp hold of your feet with your hands or with a folded towel.
3. Exhale, and pull on your feet.
4. Hold the stretch and relax.

Stretch # 50

1. Stand upright 4 or 5 steps from a wall.
2. Lean against the wall without losing the straight line of the head, neck, spine, pelvis, legs, and ankles.
3. Keep both heels down, flat, together, and parallel to the hips.
4. Exhale, bend your arms, move your chest toward the wall, and shift your weight forward.
5. Exhale, and slowly contract the quadriceps but avoid excessively jamming or locking the knee.
6. Hold the stretch and relax.

Stretch # 51

1. Stand upright, feet shoulder-width apart and toed-in, and 4 or 5 steps from a wall.
2. Lean against the wall without losing the straight line of the head, neck, spine, pelvis, legs, and ankles.
3. Keep both feet down, flat, and toed-in.
4. Exhale, bend your arms, move your chest toward the wall, and shift your weight forward.
5. Exhale, and slowly contract the quadriceps but avoid excessively jamming or locking the knee.
6. Hold the stretch and relax.

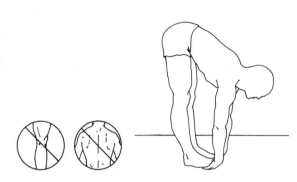

Stretch # 52

1. Stand upright with the legs straight.
2. Exhale, keeping both legs straight, extend your upper back, bend forward at the waist, and lower your hands to grasp underneath your toes.
3. Exhale, and pull up on the toes.
4. Hold the stretch and relax, but remember to either bend the knees when returning to an upright position or round the upper torso up rather than lifting with an arched back.

UPPER LEGS

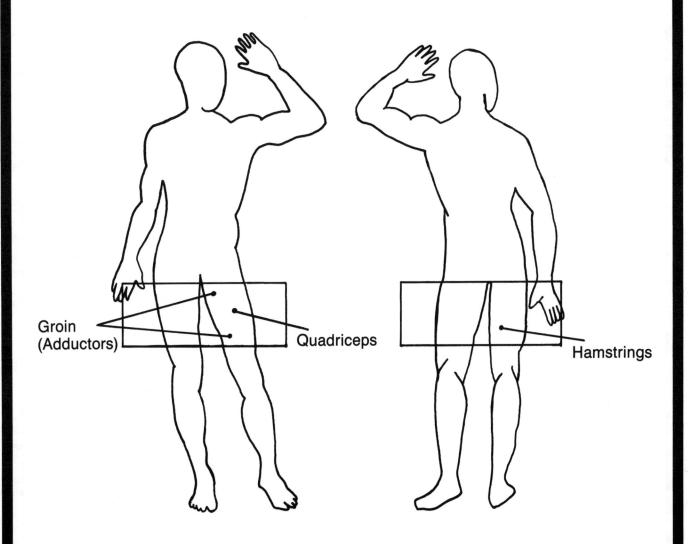

Groin
(Adductors)

Quadriceps

Hamstrings

Hamstrings

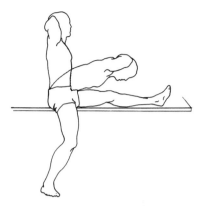

Stretch # 53 (One Leg)

1. Sit upright on the floor with both legs straight.
2. Flex your right knee and slide your heel toward your buttocks.
3. Lower the outer side of your right thigh and calf onto the floor.
4. Place your right heel against the inner side of your left thigh so that a 90-degree angle is formed between your extended left leg and flexed right leg.
5. Exhale, keeping your left leg straight, bend at the waist, and lower your extended upper torso onto your thigh.
6. Hold the stretch and relax.

Stretch # 54 (One Leg)

1. Sit upright on a bench with one leg extended and your opposite foot on the floor.
2. Exhale, extend your upper back, flex at the hips, and lower your trunk from the hips onto your thigh while keeping the leg straight.
3. Hold the stretch and relax.

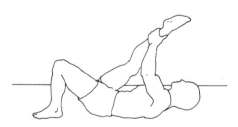

Stretch # 55 (One Leg)

1. Lie flat on your back with the legs flexed and heels close to the buttocks.
2. Inhale, and extend one leg upward.
3. Grasp underneath the leg.
4. Exhale, and slowly pull the leg toward your face while keeping the leg straight.
5. Hold the stretch and relax.

 If you have a bad back, flex the extended leg and slowly lower it to the floor.

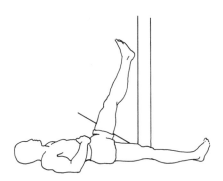

Stretch # 56 (One Leg)

1. Lie flat on your back in a doorway.
2. Position your hips slightly in front of the door frame.
3. Raise one leg and rest it against the door frame while keeping your knee extended and your bottom leg flat on the floor. To increase the stretch, slide the buttocks closer to the doorpost or lift the leg away from the door frame.
4. Hold the stretch and relax.

Stretch # 57 (One Leg)

1. Sit upright on the floor, hands behind your hips for support, and your legs extended.
2. Flex one knee and grasp the instep of your foot with one hand.
3. Exhale, and slowly extend your leg until it reaches a 90-degree angle.
4. Hold the stretch and relax.

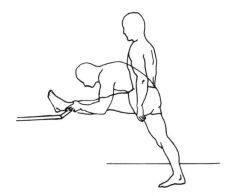

Stretch # 58 (One Leg)

1. Stand upright, slowly raise one leg, and rest it on an elevated platform at a comfortable height.
2. Exhale, keeping both legs straight and your hips squared, extend your upper back, bend forward at the waist, and lower your trunk onto your raised thigh.
3. Hold the stretch and relax.

Stretch # 59 (One Leg)

1. Assume a squat position with both hands on the floor for support and balance.
2. Inhale, and shift one foot slightly forward, placing it flat on the floor.
3. Exhale, and slowly extend your legs.
4. Hold the stretch and relax.

Stretch # 60 (One Leg)

1. Assume a squat position with your weight on the flexed right knee, the foot flat on the ground, and the left leg extended sideways.
2. Grasp the right ankle with your right hand and the left ankle with your left hand.
3. Exhale, and slowly lower your chest to your left thigh.
4. Hold the stretch and relax.

■ This exercise is considered fundamental to the martial arts. However, for most lay persons there are alternative stretches that safely accomplish the same purpose.

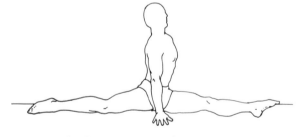
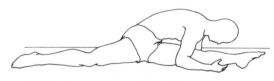

Stretch # 61 (One Leg)

1. Kneel on the floor with both legs together and your hands at your sides.
2. Lift up your left knee and place your foot a few feet in front for support.
3. Exhale, bend at the waist, lower your upper torso down onto your left thigh, and place your hands a few inches in front of your left foot for support.
4. Exhale, slowly slide your left foot forward, and straighten your legs as your rear leg is extended backward.
5. Hold the stretch and relax.

■ To perform a technically correct split, both legs must be straight, the hips squared, and the buttocks flat on the floor. For aesthetic reasons, some advocate a slight turnout of the rear hip. However, usually this is carried to an extreme, primarily due to tight hip flexors and/or improper training.

Stretch # 62 (One Leg)

1. Assume a split position.
2. Exhale, extend the upper torso, and lower your chest onto the forward thigh.
3. Hold the stretch and relax.

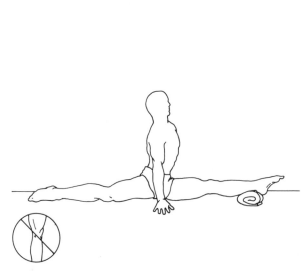

Stretch # 63 (One Leg)

1. Assume a split position with your forward leg placed on top of a folded blanket.
2. Hold the stretch and relax.

▼ This stretch should be avoided even by the vast majority of advanced athletes.

Stretch # 64 (One Leg)

1. Stand upright with your back approximately 1 foot from a wall.
2. Place your hands on the floor for balance and support as you raise one leg against the wall.
3. Exhale, and slowly slide your leg upward against the wall until you attain the split position with your legs straight and hips squared.
4. Hold the stretch and relax.

Stretch # 65 (One Leg)

1. Sit upright on the floor; flex your right leg with the outer side resting on the floor and the right heel resting against the inner side of the left thigh.
2. Your partner stands behind you with one hand on the central portion of your upper back and the other hand on the central portion of your lower back.
3. Exhale. Keeping your forward leg straight, extend your upper back, bend forward at the waist, and allow your partner to assist in gently pushing your upper torso onto your thigh. Communicate with your partner and use great care.
4. Hold the stretch and relax.

Stretch # 66 (One Leg)

1. Sit upright on the floor; flex your left leg with the outer side resting on the floor and the left heel resting against the inner side of the right thigh.
2. Your partner assumes the same position.
3. Your extended leg will brace against your partner's flexed leg and vice versa.
4. Interlock hands.
5. Exhale. Keeping your forward leg straight, extend your upper back, bend forward at the waist, and lower your trunk onto your thigh as your partner leans backward and pulls on your hands. Communicate with your partner and use great care.
6. Hold the stretch and relax.

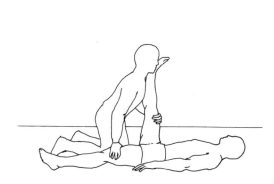

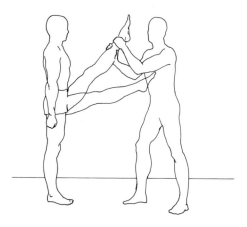

Stretch # 67 (One Leg)

1. Lie flat on your back with your body straight.
2. Inhale, raise one leg, and keep your hips square.
3. Your partner anchors your lower leg and grasps your raised leg.
4. Exhale slowly as your partner raises your leg. (Both legs must remain straight and your hips must be kept squared.) Communicate with your partner and use great care.
5. Hold the stretch and relax.

Stretch # 68 (One Leg)

1. Stand upright facing your partner and holding onto a surface for balance and support.
2. Inhale, raise one leg, and keep your hips squared.
3. Your partner grasps your raised leg with both hands above your ankle.
4. Exhale as your partner slowly raises your leg. (Both legs must remain straight and your hips must be kept squared.) Communicate with your partner and use great care.
5. Hold the stretch and relax.

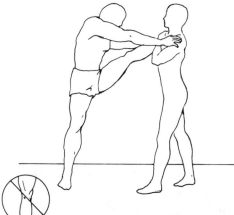

Stretch # 69 (One Leg)

1. Stand upright facing your partner.
2. Place your leg on your partner's shoulder.
3. Exhale, and bend forward to your knee as your partner steps backward. Communicate with your partner and use great care.
4. Hold the stretch and relax.

■ This stretch is commonly cited in martial arts texts. However, it is unnecessary for even most advanced athletes.

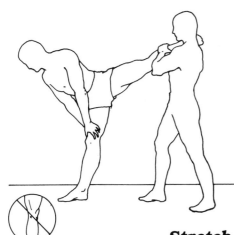

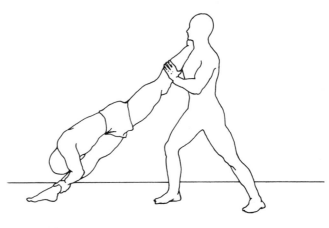

Stretch # 70 (One Leg)

1. Stand upright facing your partner.
2. Place your leg on your partner's shoulder.
3. Turn away from your partner.
4. Exhale, and lean slowly forward toward your ankle as your partner steps backward. Communicate with your partner and use great care.
5. Hold the stretch and relax.

■ This stretch is commonly cited in martial arts texts. However, it is unnecessary for even most advanced athletes.

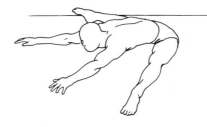

Stretch # 71

1. Sit upright on the floor with both legs extended.
2. Exhale, keeping both legs straight, extend your upper back, bend forward at the waist, and lower your trunk onto your thighs. Stop when you feel excess tension.
3. Hold the stretch and relax.

Stretch # 72

1. Sit upright on the floor with both legs extended.
2. Straddle your legs.
3. Exhale, keeping both legs straight, extend your upper back, bend forward from the waist, and lower your trunk onto the floor.
4. Hold the stretch and relax.

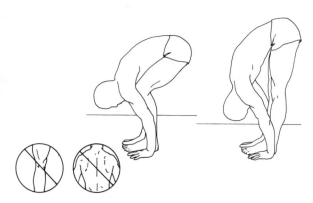

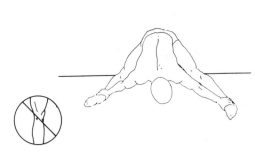

Stretch # 73

1. Assume a squat position with your chest on your thighs and your hands resting on the floor.
2. Exhale, and slowly extend your legs. Stop when you feel excess tension.
3. Hold the stretch and relax.
4. Flex the knees and return to the starting position.

Stretch # 74

1. Assume a squat position with your legs straddled wide and your hands grasping the ankles or feet.
2. Exhale, and slowly extend your legs.
3. Exhale, and slowly pull your chest closer to the legs.
4. Hold the stretch and relax.
5. Flex the knees and return to the starting position.

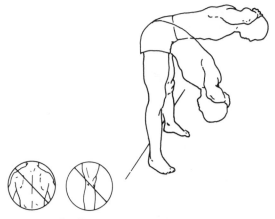

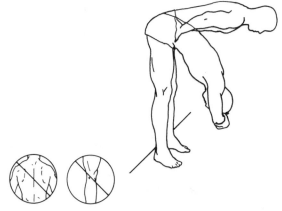

Stretch # 75

1. Stand upright, legs straddled, and with the back of your heels 6 inches from a wall.
2. Interlock your hands behind your head.
3. Exhale, keeping both legs straight, extend your upper back, bend forward at the waist, and lower your trunk toward your thighs.
4. Hold the stretch and relax.
5. Exhale, and either bend the knees or round the upper torso up rather than lifting with an arched back when returning to an upright position.

Stretch # 76

1. Stand upright with the back of your heels almost together and 6 inches from a wall and with both hands on your hips.
2. Raise both arms and interlock your hands behind your head.
3. Exhale, keeping both legs straight, extend your upper back, bend forward at the waist, and lower your trunk onto your thighs.
4. Hold the stretch and relax.
5. Exhale, and either bend the knees or round the upper torso up rather than lifting with an arched back when returning to an upright position.

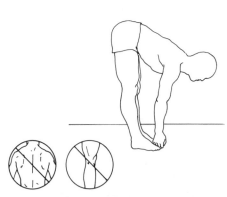

Stretch # 77

1. Stand upright with your feet together.
2. Exhale, keeping both legs straight, extend your upper back, bend forward at the waist, and touch your toes.
3. Hold the stretch and relax.
4. Exhale, and either bend the knees or round the upper torso up rather than lifting with an arched back when returning to an upright position.

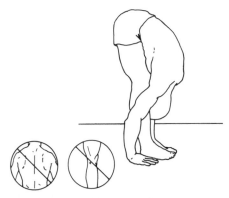

Stretch # 78

1. Stand upright with your feet together.
2. Exhale, keeping both legs straight, extend your upper back, bend forward at the waist, lower your trunk onto your thighs, and place your hands flat on the floor.
3. Hold the stretch and relax.
4. Exhale, and either bend the knees or round the upper torso up rather than lifting with an arched back when returning to an upright position.

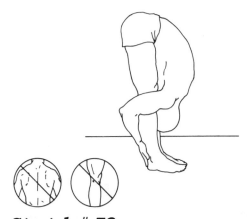

Stretch # 79

1. Stand upright with your feet together.
2. Exhale, keeping both legs straight, extend your upper back, bend forward at the waist, lower your trunk onto your thighs, and grasp the backs of your ankles.
3. Exhale, and compress your chest to your thighs.
4. Hold the stretch and relax.
5. Exhale, and either bend the knees or round the upper torso up rather than lifting with an arched back when returning to an upright position.

Stretch # 80

1. Sit upright on the floor with your legs extended.
2. Your partner assumes the same position, with feet braced against yours.
3. You and your partner hold onto a folded towel.
4. Exhale. Keeping your legs straight, extend the upper back, bend forward at the waist, and lower your trunk onto your thighs as your partner *slowly* leans backward and pulls on the towel. Communicate with your partner and use great care.
5. Hold the stretch and relax.

Stretch # 81

1. Sit upright on the floor with your legs extended.
2. Your partner stands behind you with one hand on the central portion of your upper back and the other on the central portion of your lower back.
3. Exhale. Keeping your legs straight, extend your upper back, bend forward at the waist, and allow your partner to assist in *slowly* pushing your upper torso onto your thighs. Communicate with your partner and use great care.
4. Hold the stretch and relax.

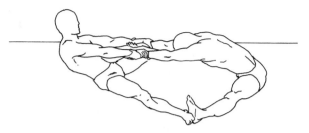

Stretch # 82

1. Sit upright on the floor with your legs straight and straddled.
2. Your partner assumes the same position with feet braced against yours.
3. Lean forward and grasp each other's wrists.
4. Exhale. Keeping your legs straight, extend your upper back, bend forward at the waist as your partner *slowly* leans backward and pulls on your hands. Communicate with your partner and use great care.
5. Hold the stretch and relax.

Stretch # 83

1. Sit upright on the floor with your legs straight and straddled.
2. Your partner stands behind you with both hands on the central portion of your lower back.
3. Exhale. Keeping your legs straight, extend your upper back, lean forward at the waist, and allow your partner to assist in *slowly* pushing your upper torso onto the floor. Communicate with your partner and use great care.
4. Hold the stretch and relax.

Stretch # 84

1. Stand upright, feet about shoulder-width apart, holding a light barbell across your shoulders.
2. Inhale, and with the legs straight, bend over so your chest is parallel to the floor.
3. Hold the stretch and relax.
4. Exhale and return to an erect position.

■ Some athletes perform the "Good Morning" exercise with the legs slightly flexed when using heavier weights. Here, the objective is to develop greater lower back strength. Regardless of the technique used, it is strongly recommended that a lifting belt be worn with this controversial stretch.

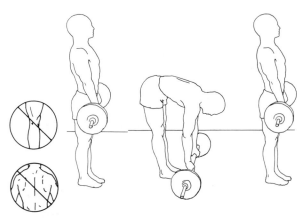

Stretch # 85

1. Stand upright holding a light barbell.
2. Inhale, and with the legs straight, bend forward at the waist and lower the barbell to the floor.
3. Hold the stretch momentarily.
4. Exhale, and slowly return to an upright position with the legs kept straight.

■ As your flexibility increases, you may want to do "dead lifts" while standing on the end of a bench or large block. It is strongly recommended that a lifting belt be worn with this controversial stretch.

Adductors

Stretch # 86

1. Sit upright on the floor.
2. Flex your knees and bring the heels and soles of your feet together as you pull them toward your buttocks.
3. Place your elbows on the inside portion of both upper legs.
4. Exhale, and slowly push your legs to the floor.
5. Hold the stretch and relax.

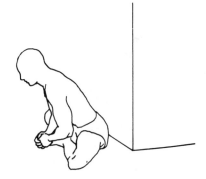

Stretch # 87

1. Sit upright on the floor with your legs flexed and straddled and heels touching each other.
2. Grasp your feet or ankles and pull them as close to your buttocks as possible.
3. Exhale, lean forward from the hips without bending your back, and attempt to lower your chest to the floor.
4. Hold the stretch and relax.

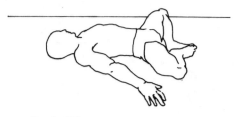

Stretch # 88

1. Lie flat on your back with your body straight.
2. Flex your knees and bring the heels and soles of your feet together as you pull them toward your buttocks.
3. Exhale, and straddle your knees as wide as possible with the soles of your feet remaining in contact.
4. Hold the stretch and relax.

Stretch # 89

1. Lie flat on your back; flex and straddle your legs with the heels and soles of your feet touching each other and resting against a wall.
2. Place your hands on the upper inside portions of your legs.
3. Exhale, and slowly straddle your legs as wide as possible.
4. Hold the stretch and relax.

 Move farther from the wall if you feel pressure building in your lower back.

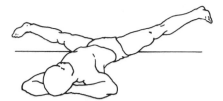

Stretch # 90

1. Lie flat on your back with your legs raised and together and your buttocks several inches from a wall.
2. Exhale, and slowly straddle your legs as wide as possible. (Wear shoes to intensify the stretch.)
3. Hold the stretch and relax.

Stretch # 91

1. Sit upright on the floor with both legs straight.
2. Straddle your legs as wide as possible.
3. Exhale, rotate your trunk, and extend your upper torso onto your leg. Concentrate on keeping both the lower back and the legs extended.
4. Hold the stretch and relax.

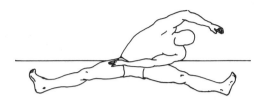

Stretch # 92

1. Sit upright on the floor with both legs straight.
2. Straddle your legs as wide as possible.
3. Drop one arm and raise your other arm overhead.
4. Exhale, rotate your trunk, and extend your upper torso onto your leg.
5. Hold the stretch and relax.

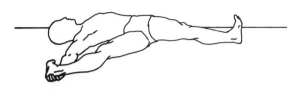

Stretch # 93

1. Lie flat on your back with your body straight.
2. Flex one leg, grasp the foot, and extend the leg vertically.
3. Exhale, and slowly lower your leg to the floor at your side forming the letter Y.
4. Hold the stretch and relax.

Stretch # 94

1. Kneel on all fours with your toes facing backward.
2. Extend one leg out sideways.
3. Exhale, bend your arms, lower the hip of the opposing side to the floor, and roll the hip.
4. Hold the stretch and relax.

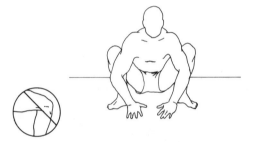

Stretch # 95

1. Assume a squat position with your feet about 12 inches apart and your toes turned slightly out.
2. Place your elbows on the inside portions of your upper legs.
3. Exhale, and slowly push your legs outward with your elbows. Remember to keep your feet flat on the floor to reduce strain on the knees.
4. Hold the stretch and relax.

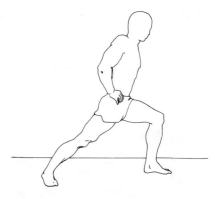

Stretch # 96

1. Kneel on all fours with your toes facing backward.
2. Bend your arms and rest your elbows on the floor.
3. Exhale, slowly straddle your knees, and attempt to lower your chest to the floor.
4. Hold the stretch and relax.

 This is one of the most intense stretches for the adductors—it's extremely deceptive.

Stretch # 97

1. Stand upright with your legs straddled about 2 feet apart.
2. Turn the left foot 90 degrees sideways to the left, keeping the toes and heel in line with the body.
3. Place your hands on your hips.
4. Exhale, slowly lunge forward, and press down on your right hip.
5. Hold the stretch and relax.

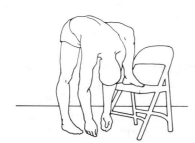

Stretch # 98

1. Stand upright with one leg raised and the foot resting on the seat of a chair.
2. Exhale, bend at the waist, and lower your hands toward the floor.
3. Hold the stretch and relax.
4. Exhale, and bend the knee or round the upper torso when returning to the upright position.

Stretch # 99

1. Stand upright facing a barre.
2. Inhale, raise one leg to the supporting surface, and place your heel or instep on top.
3. Exhale, and slowly slide your foot along the surface.
4. Hold the stretch and relax.

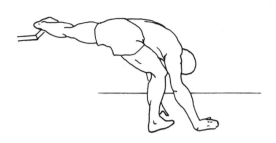

Stretch # 100

1. Stand upright, feet parallel to a supporting surface.
2. Inhale, raise one leg to the supporting surface, and place your heel or instep on top.
3. Raise your arms overhead and interlock your hands.
4. Exhale. Keeping your legs straight, bend sideways and lower your upper torso toward your raised thigh.
5. Hold the stretch and relax.

Stretch # 101

1. Stand upright, feet parallel to a supporting surface.
2. Keeping both legs straight and your hips squared, raise one leg and place your heel on the supporting surface.
3. Turn out the foot of the supporting leg.
4. Roll your hips and turn the raised leg medially.
5. Exhale. Keeping the raised leg straight, flex the supporting leg, and lower your chest to your knee.
6. Hold the stretch and relax.

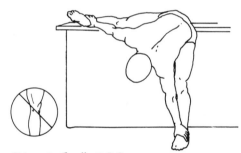

Stretch # 102

1. Stand upright, feet parallel to a supporting surface.
2. Keeping both legs straight and your hips squared, raise one leg and place your heel on the supporting surface.
3. Turn out the foot of the supporting leg.
4. Roll your hips and turn the raised leg medially.
5. Grasp the raised foot with one hand.
6. Exhale, bend forward at the waist, and grasp the foot of the supporting leg.
7. Exhale, keep both legs straight, and lower your upper torso as if performing a straddle split.
8. Hold the stretch and relax.

Stretch # 103

1. Stand upright.
2. Draw the toe of one foot to the opposite ankle and slide it up the inside of your leg to your knee.
3. Grasp the foot with your hand.
4. Inhale, and slowly raise and straighten your leg sideways.
5. Hold the stretch and relax.

■ Dancers are capable of performing this skill without the use of their arms for support. For most people, a lack of coordination or strength in the hip flexors will be the chief limiting factor.

Stretch # 104

1. Sit upright with your legs straddled and straight.
2. Exhale, and slowly lower your chest and belly onto the floor while keeping your back flat.
3. Hold the stretch and relax.

■ Ideally, your legs should form a straight line when executing a straddle or Japanese split. Those with greater flexibility can roll the hips forward and backward.

Stretch # 105

1. Sit upright on the floor.
2. Flex your knees and bring the heels and soles of your feet together as you pull them toward your buttocks.
3. Your partner faces you with his or her hands on the inside portions of your upper legs.
4. Exhale, and allow your partner to assist you in lowering your legs to the floor. Communicate with your partner and use great care.
5. Hold the stretch and relax.

Stretch # 106

1. Lie flat on your back with your body straight.
2. Flex your knees and bring the heels and soles of your feet together as you pull them toward your buttocks.
3. Your partner kneels on the floor facing you with his or her hands on your knees.
4. Exhale as you allow your partner to gently push your legs to the floor. Communicate with your partner and use great care.
5. Hold the stretch and relax.

Stretch # 107

1. Lie flat on your back; flex and straddle your legs with the heels and soles of your feet touching each other and resting against a wall.
2. Your partner stands facing you with his or her hands on the upper inside portion of your legs.
3. Exhale as you allow your partner to gently push your legs to the floor. Communicate with your partner and use great care.
4. Hold the stretch and relax.

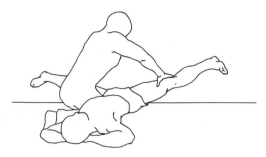

Stretch # 108

1. Lie flat on your back with your legs raised and together, and your buttocks several inches from a wall.
2. Exhale, and slowly straddle your legs as wide as possible.
3. Your partner kneels facing you and grasps the inside of your thighs.
4. Exhale as you allow your partner to gently straddle the legs farther while keeping both legs straight. Communicate with your partner and use great care.
5. Hold the stretch and relax.

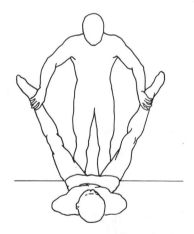

Stretch # 109

1. Lie flat on your back with both legs raised vertically and straddled.
2. Your partner stands facing you and grasping both ankles or lower legs.
3. Exhale, as you allow your partner to gently straddle the legs farther. Communicate with your partner and use great care.
4. Hold the stretch and relax.

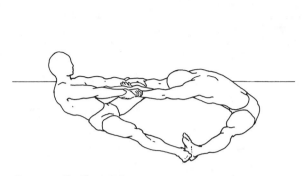

Stretch # 110

1. Sit upright on the floor with your legs straddled and straight.
2. Your partner assumes the same position. Brace your feet together, and interlock hands.
3. Exhale. Keeping your legs straight, bend at the waist, and lower your upper torso toward the floor as your partner leans backward and pulls on your hands. Communicate with your partner and use great care.
4. Hold the stretch and relax.

Stretch # 111

1. Sit upright on the floor with your legs straddled.
2. Your partner kneels facing you and grasps your ankles or shins.
3. Exhale as you allow your partner to gently straddle your legs farther. Communicate with your partner and use great care.
4. Hold the stretch and relax.

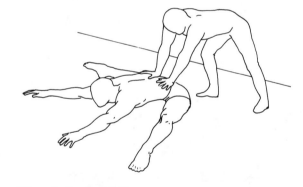

Stretch # 112

1. Sit upright with your legs straight and straddled.
2. Your partner stands behind you with his or her hands on the center of your back.
3. Exhale as you allow your partner to gently push your upper torso onto the floor. Communicate with your partner and use great care. Extend from the hips, and do not round your upper back.
4. Hold the stretch and relax.

Stretch # 113

1. Kneel on all fours with your legs straddled.
2. Your partner kneels either to your side or directly behind you and places his or her hands on your buttocks and upper back.
3. Exhale as you allow your partner to gently push down to further straddle your knees. Use exceptional care with this super stretch!
4. Hold the stretch and relax.

Stretch # 114

1. Kneel on all fours with your toes facing backward.
2. Your partner is positioned on your right side.
3. Your partner slides his or her right leg between your legs through the groin and hooks your right ankle or leg (Grapevine).
4. Your partner reaches across your lower back and grasps your left knee with his or her hands.
5. Your partner pulls up your left knee from the floor and rolls to his or her right with you following. When the roll is completed, your partner will be on his or her back with your back and buttocks on his or her stomach and your legs straddled. If necessary, your partner can then hook the left foot over your right foot.
6. Exhale as you allow your partner to gently pull your legs farther apart.
7. Hold the stretch and relax.

 Extreme caution must be used with this super stretch. Furthermore, when executing the "banana split" make sure your left knee is completely flexed to avoid excessive stress on the medial part of the knee.

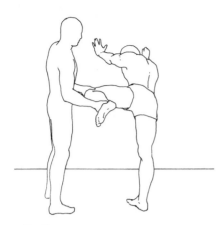

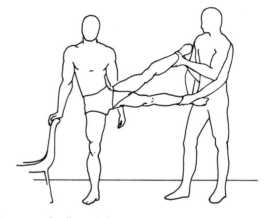

Stretch # 115

1. Stand upright with your hands resting on a wall.
2. Inhale, flex your knee, and raise it sideways.
3. Your partner is standing to your side and grasps the ankle and knee.
4. Exhale as you allow your partner to gently raise your leg farther. Communicate with your partner and use great care.
5. Hold the stretch and relax.

Stretch # 116

1. Stand upright and raise one leg sideways.
2. Your partner is positioned to your side, holding your heel with one hand and above your ankle with the other hand.
3. Exhale as you allow your partner to gently raise your legs. Communicate with your partner and use great care. Concentrate on preventing your buttocks from protruding. You might find it easier if you hold onto a surface for additional support and balance.
4. Hold the stretch and relax.

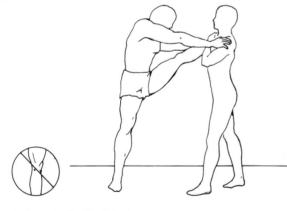

Stretch # 117

1. Stand upright facing your partner.
2. Place your leg on your partner's shoulder.
3. Turn your hip so your feet face away from your partner.
4. Exhale as your partner slowly steps away from you. Communicate with your partner and use great care.
5. Hold the stretch and relax.

■ This is another of those stretches used in the martial arts. Once again, it is of doubtful value for the vast majority of even elite athletes. Safer alternatives exist for us mere mortals!

Stretch # 118

1. Stand upright while holding a pair of dumbbells.
2. Inhale, and lower your body until one knee rests on the floor.
3. Hold the stretch and relax.
4. Exhale, and return to the starting position. Use a light weight to start, and do not lift the heel of your leading foot or allow your knee to go past your toes.

Stretch # 119

1. Stand upright with your feet parallel and shoulder-width apart and a light barbell resting across your shoulders.
2. Inhale, and lower your body until one knee rests on the floor.
3. Hold the stretch and relax.
4. Exhale, and return to the starting position. Use a light weight to start, and do not lift the heel of your leading foot or allow your knee to go past your toes.

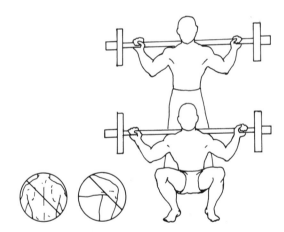

Stretch # 120

1. Stand upright with your feet about shoulder-width apart and with a light barbell across your shoulders.
2. Inhale, and slowly lower your buttocks toward the floor while keeping heels flat on the floor.
3. Hold the stretch at the bottom.
4. Exhale, and return to the starting position.

 This stretch is very controversial. Always use a light weight that can be handled easily. The use of a lifting belt to provide extra support is strongly recommended.

Quadriceps

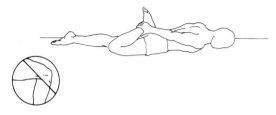

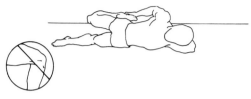

Stretch # 121 (One Leg)

1. Lie face down with your body extended.
2. Flex one leg and bring your heel toward your buttocks.
3. Exhale, swing your arm back to grasp your ankle, and pull your heel toward your buttocks without overcompressing the knee.
4. Hold the stretch and relax.

Stretch # 122 (One Leg)

1. Lie on your side.
2. Flex one leg and bring your heel toward your buttocks.
3. Exhale, swing your arm back to grasp your ankle, and pull your heel toward your buttocks without overcompressing the knee.
4. Hold the stretch and relax.

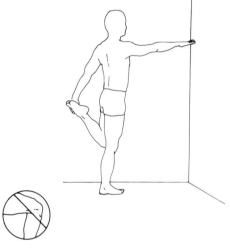

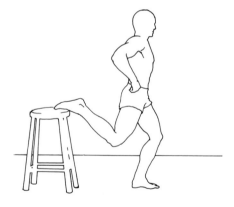

Stretch # 123 (One Leg)

1. Stand upright with one hand against a surface for balance and support.
2. Flex one leg and raise the foot to your buttocks.
3. Slightly flex the supporting leg.
4. Exhale, reach down, grasp your raised foot with one hand, and pull your heel toward your buttocks without over-compressing the knee.
5. Hold the stretch and relax.

Stretch # 124 (One Leg)

1. Stand upright with the top of one foot resting on a chair or low stand behind you.
2. Exhale, and flex the front knee.
3. Hold the stretch and relax.

Stretch # 125 (One Leg)

1. Lie on your back at the edge of a table, with your left side toward the edge.
2. Exhale, slowly lower your left leg off the table, and grasp the ankle or foot with your left hand.
3. Inhale, and slowly pull your heel toward your buttocks.
4. Hold the stretch and relax.

▼ You might need an assistant if you are very tight. Also, to protect your lower back, lift up your head and contract the abdominal muscles.

Stretch # 126 (One Leg)

1. Lie on your back at the edge of a table with your left side toward the edge.
2. Flex your right leg and slide it toward the buttocks to help anchor and stabilize your hips.
3. Grasp your leg under the right thigh with your right hand.
4. Exhale, slowly lower your left leg off the table, and grasp the ankle or foot with your left hand.
5. Inhale, and slowly pull your left heel toward your buttocks.
6. Hold the stretch and relax.

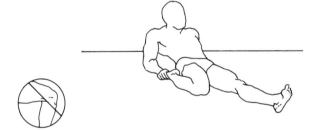

Stretch # 127 (One Leg)

1. Sit upright on the floor with both legs extended.
2. Bend your right leg behind you so that the insides of the knee and thigh are on the floor and the foot points along the line of the lower leg in a relaxed position.
3. Exhale, and slowly lean diagonally back onto your forearm and elbow opposite your rear leg without arching your lower back.
4. Exhale, and continue leaning backward until you are flat on your back.
5. Hold the stretch and relax.

 Do not let the foot of the rear leg flare out to the side. This will protect the knee. To guard against excessive stress on the lumbar spine, keep your forward leg in a slightly flexed position. However, to increase the stretch, just contract the buttock muscles and lift the hip off the floor.

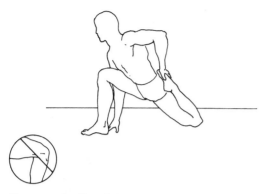

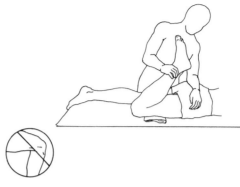

Stretch # 128 (One Leg)

1. Assume a squat position with both hands on the floor for support and one leg resting on the floor.
2. Inhale, lift up your buttocks, and extend your rear leg backward.
3. Inhale, and flex your rear leg up to your buttocks.
4. Reach back and grasp your rear foot.
5. Exhale, and slowly pull your heel toward your buttocks.
6. Hold the stretch and relax.

■ An easier and less stressful variation is to apply the stretch with one elbow and the opposite leg resting on the floor. Thus, you would simply start from a kneeling position.

Stretch # 129 (One Leg)

1. Lie face down with one leg flexed toward your buttocks.
2. Your partner is positioned at your side with one hand anchoring your hips and the other grasping your ankle.
3. Exhale as you allow your partner to push your heel toward your buttocks.
4. Hold the stretch and relax.

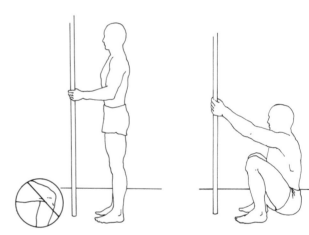

Stretch # 130 (One Leg)

1. Lie on a bench or table with your left leg flexed behind you so that the insides of the knee and thigh are resting on the surface and the foot points toward your left shoulder.
2. Your partner is positioned either kneeling or standing at your side with one hand anchoring your hip and the other hand on your knee.
3. Exhale as you allow your partner to gently push down on your hip and knee.
4. Hold the stretch and relax.

Stretch # 131

1. Stand upright holding a pole, with your feet parallel about 1 foot apart.
2. Inhale, and lower your buttocks to the floor, keeping the back straight and the heels flat on the floor.
3. Hold the stretch and relax.
4. Exhale, and return to the starting position.

Stretch # 132

1. Kneel on all fours with your toes facing backward. (If this is uncomfortable, place a blanket underneath your shins.)
2. Exhale, and slowly sit on your heels (if you can).
3. Hold the stretch and relax.

Stretch # 133

1. Kneel upright with knees together, buttocks on the floor, heels by the side of your thighs, and toes pointing backward.
2. Exhale and slowly lean backward without letting your feet flare out to the sides.
3. Hold the stretch and relax.

Stretch # 134

1. Kneel upright with knees together, buttocks on the floor, heels by the side of your thighs, and toes pointing backward.
2. Exhale as you continue leaning backward until you are flat on your back. Do not let your feet flare out to the sides.
3. Hold the stretch and relax.

HIPS, BUTTOCKS, AND ABDOMEN

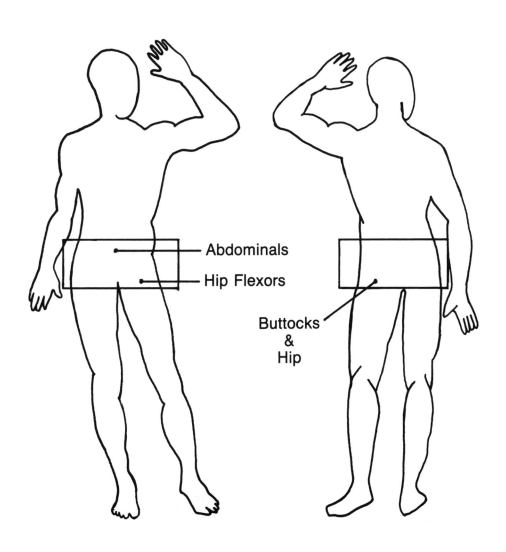

Abdominals

Hip Flexors

Buttocks
&
Hip

Hip Flexors

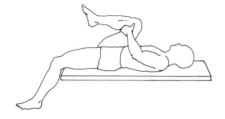

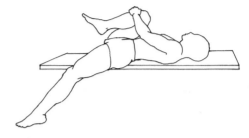

Stretch # 135

1. Lie on a table, flat on your back, with both legs hanging over the edge.
2. Inhale, flex one knee, and raise it to your chest.
3. Interlock your hands behind the raised knee.
4. Inhale, and pull your knee to your chest as you keep the opposite leg hanging over the edge.
5. Hold the stretch and relax.

Stretch # 136

1. Lie on a table, flat on your back, by the edge.
2. Allow one of your legs to hang over the side.
3. Inhale, flex the opposite knee, grasp it with your hands, and bring it to your chest.
4. Inhale, and compress your thigh to your chest.
5. Hold the stretch and relax.

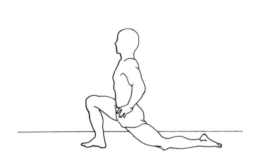

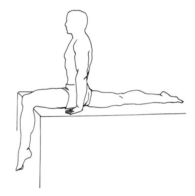

Stretch # 137

1. Stand upright with the legs straddled 2 feet apart.
2. Turn your right foot 90 degrees sideways to the right, keeping your toes and heel in line with your body.
3. Flex your right knee, and roll your left foot under so the top of the instep rests on the floor.
4. Place your hands on your hips. (Some may prefer placing one hand on the forward knee and one hand on the buttocks.)
5. Exhale, and slowly lean or push your left hip toward the floor.
6. Hold the stretch and relax.

Stretch # 138

1. Sit upright on an elevated platform (pile of mats or a bed) about 3 feet above the floor.
2. Position your left leg so it drops over the edge of the platform at the knee, and swing your right leg back so it assumes a split position with your leg (thigh, knee, shinbone, and ankle) resting on the platform.
3. Exhale, and slowly push down on the platform with both hands, keeping your hips squared and turned under.
4. Hold the stretch and relax.

Stretch # 139

1. Sit upright on an elevated platform (pile of mats or a bed) about 3 feet above the floor.
2. Position your right leg so it drops over the edge of the platform at the knee, and swing your left leg back so it assumes a split position with your leg (thigh, knee, shinbone, and ankle) resting on the platform.
3. Inhale, and flex your rear leg up to your buttocks.
4. Reach back and grasp your foot.
5. Exhale, and slowly pull your heel toward your buttocks.
6. Hold the stretch and relax.

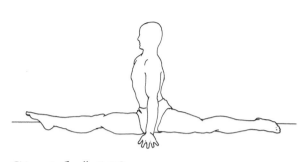

Stretch # 140

1. Kneel on the floor with both legs together and your hands at your sides.
2. Lift your right knee and place your foot a few feet in front for support.
3. Exhale, bend at the waist, lower your upper torso onto your right thigh, and place your hands a few inches in front of your right foot for support.
4. Exhale, slowly sliding your right foot forward, and straighten your legs as your rear leg is extended backward.
5. Hold the stretch and relax.

■ To perform a technically correct split, both legs must be straight, the hips squared, and the buttocks flat on the floor.

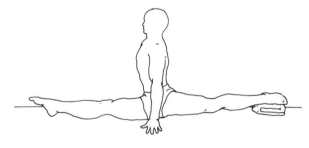

Stretch # 141

1. Assume a split position with your rear leg elevated on a folded mat.
2. Hold the stretch and relax.

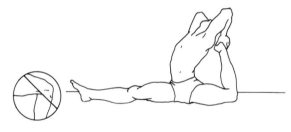

Stretch # 142

1. Assume a split position.
2. Inhale, and flex your rear leg up toward your buttocks.
3. Reach back and grasp your foot.
4. Exhale, and slowly pull your heel toward your buttocks.
5. Hold the stretch and relax.

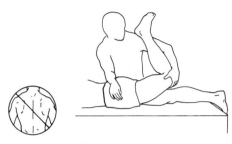

Stretch # 143

1. Stand upright with your back approximately 1 foot from a wall.
2. Place your hands on the floor for balance and support as you raise one leg against the wall.
3. Exhale, and slowly slide your leg upward against the wall until you attain the split position with your legs straight and hips squared.
4. Hold the stretch and relax.

Stretch # 144

1. Lie face down with your body extended.
2. Your partner is positioned at your side, standing or resting on one knee, with one hand under your knee and the other slightly above the buttocks.
3. Inhale, and contract your gluteals (buttock muscles) as you allow your partner to anchor down your belly to the table or floor with one hand and gently lift your leg higher with the opposite hand. Communicate with your partner and use great care.
4. Hold the stretch and relax.

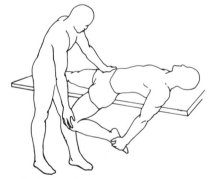

Stretch # 145

1. Lie flat on your back at the edge of a table with your left side toward the edge.
2. Exhale, and slowly lower your left leg off the table and grasp the ankle or foot with your left hand.
3. Your partner stands at your side with one hand on your left knee and the other on your right hip.
4. Exhale as you allow your partner to gently press down on the hip and knee. Communicate with your partner and use great care.
5. Hold the stretch and relax.

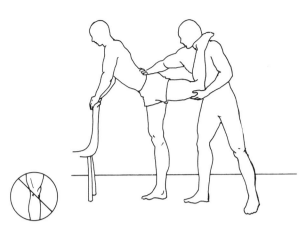

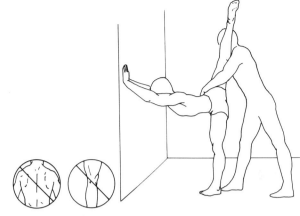

Stretch # 146

1. Stand upright with a slight turnout on the foot to balance on, and holding onto a surface for balance and support.
2. Exhale, bend at your waist, flex one knee, and raise your leg.
3. Your partner stands behind you with one hand under your knee and the other hand slightly above your buttocks.
4. Inhale as you allow your partner to anchor down your body with one hand and lift your raised leg with the opposite hand.
5. Hold the stretch and relax.

▼ Hyperextension of the back when performing an arabesque can be a potential source of pain and injury. Here, the answer is to spread the extension through all the joints of the spine, instead of forcing it all at the bottom of the spine.

Stretch # 147

1. Assume an arabesque position (as in stretch #146), but keep your raised leg straight.
2. Your partner stands behind you and rests your raised thigh on his or her shoulder.
3. Your partner reaches over your raised leg, interlocks his or her fingers, and places his or her hands on your upper buttocks.
4. Inhale as you allow your partner to anchor down your body with one hand and raise your extended thigh up and forward with his or her shoulder.
5. Hold the stretch and relax.

▼ Hyperextension of the back when performing an arabesque can be a potential source of pain and injury. Here, the answer is to spread the extension through all the joints of the spine, instead of forcing it all at the bottom of the spine.

Buttocks and Hips

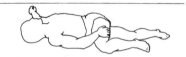

Stretch # 148

1. Lie flat on your back with your legs extended.
2. Flex one knee and raise it to your chest.
3. Grasp your knee or thigh with one hand.
4. Exhale, and pull your knee across your body to the floor while keeping your elbows, head, and shoulders flat on the floor.
5. Hold the stretch and relax.

Stretch # 149

1. Lie flat on your back with one leg raised and straight and your arms out to your sides.
2. Exhale, and slowly lower your raised leg to the opposite hand while keeping your elbows, head, and shoulders flat on the floor.
3. Hold the stretch and relax.

Stretch # 150

1. Lie flat on your back on the edge of a table, with one leg raised and straight and your arms out to the sides.
2. Exhale, and slowly lower your raised leg to the opposite hand.
3. Exhale, and pull on your hanging leg with the opposite hand while keeping your head and shoulders flat on the table.
4. Hold the stretch and relax.

Stretch # 151

1. Lie flat on your back with your knees flexed and your hands interlocked underneath your head.
2. Lift your left leg over your right leg and hook your leg.
3. Exhale, and use your left leg to press your right leg to the floor while keeping your elbows, head, and shoulders flat on the floor.
4. Hold the stretch and relax.

Stretch # 152

1. Lie flat on your back with your left leg crossed over your right knee.
2. Inhale, flex your right knee, and let it push your left foot toward your face while keeping your head, shoulders, and back flat on the floor.
3. Hold the stretch and relax.

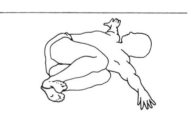

Stretch # 153

1. Lie flat on your back with your knees flexed and arms out to the sides.
2. Exhale, and slowly lower both legs to the floor on the same side while keeping your elbows, head, and shoulders flat on the floor.
3. Hold the stretch and relax.

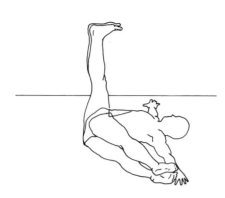

Stretch # 154

1. Lie flat on your back with your legs raised and straight and your arms out to the sides.
2. Exhale, and slowly lower both legs to the floor on the same side while keeping your elbows, head, and shoulders flat on the floor.
3. Hold the stretch and relax.

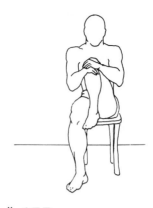

Stretch # 155

1. Sit upright on a chair with one leg flexed and the heel resting on the chair edge.
2. Interlock both hands and grasp your raised knee.
3. Exhale, and slowly pull your knee to your body as your heel remains flat on the chair.
4. Hold the stretch and relax.

Stretch # 156

1. Sit upright on the floor with hands behind your hips for support and your legs extended.
2. Flex your left leg, cross your left foot over your right leg, and slide your heel toward your buttocks.
3. Reach over your left leg with your right arm, and place your right elbow on the outside of your left knee.
4. Exhale, and look over your left shoulder while turning your trunk and pushing back on your knee with your right elbow.
5. Hold the stretch and relax.

Stretch # 157

1. Lie on your side with knees and hips extended in a straight line with your trunk.
2. Exhale and push up to a resting position on your hip, placing your arm directly under your shoulder and bearing weight on your extended arm and hand. (It may be necessary to place the opposite foot on the floor to stabilize the pelvis.)
3. Hold the stretch and relax.

Stretch # 158

1. Sit upright in a chair or on the floor with one leg crossed over the opposite knee.
2. Place your hand on the medial part of your knee.
3. Exhale and slowly lean forward.
4. Hold the stretch and relax.

Stretch # 159

1. Sit upright on the floor, resting your left leg in front of you with your knee flexed and your foot pointing to the right.
2. Cross your right leg over your left leg and place the foot flat on the floor.
3. Exhale, round your upper torso, and bend forward.
4. Hold the stretch and relax.

Stretch # 160

1. Sit upright on the floor.
2. Cross one knee over the other.
3. Exhale and lean forward.
4. Hold the stretch and relax.

Stretch # 161

1. Lie on the floor with your body extended.
2. Flex one leg and slide the heel toward your buttocks.
3. Grasp the ankle with one hand and the knee with the opposite hand.
4. Exhale, and slowly pull your foot to the opposite shoulder while keeping your head, shoulders, and back flat on the floor.
5. Hold the stretch and relax.

Stretch # 162

1. Sit upright on the floor with your back flat against a wall.
2. Flex one leg and slide the heel toward your buttocks.
3. Grasp the ankle with one hand and hook the knee with the elbow of your opposite shoulder.
4. Exhale, and slowly pull your foot to the opposite shoulder.
5. Hold the stretch and relax.

Stretch # 163

1. Kneel on all fours.
2. Exhale, flex one arm, and slowly rotate your hip out to that side.
3. Hold the stretch and relax.

Stretch # 164

1. Stand upright with your feet together and your side to a wall about an arm's length away.
2. Place one hand on the wall and the heel of your other hand on the back of your hip joint.
3. Exhale. Keeping your legs straight, contract your buttocks and rotate your hips slightly forward and in toward the wall.
4. Exhale, and push your hip toward the wall.
5. Hold the stretch and relax.

Stretch # 165

1. Stand upright 4 or 5 steps from a wall.
2. Bend one leg forward and keep the opposite leg straight.
3. Lean against the wall without losing the straight line of the head, neck, spine, pelvis, rear leg, and ankle.
4. Keep your rear heel down, flat, and parallel to the hips.
5. Exhale, and slowly rotate the hip of the rear leg out sideways.
6. Hold the stretch and relax.

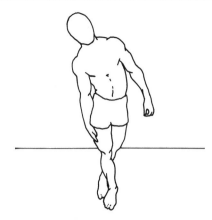

Stretch # 166

1. Stand upright with your hands at your sides.
2. Extend and adduct your left leg as far as possible.
3. Exhale, and slowly flex your trunk laterally toward your right side with your hands remaining by your hips.
4. Hold the stretch and relax.

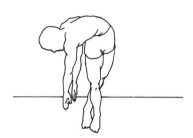

Stretch # 167

1. Stand upright with your hands at your sides.
2. Extend and adduct your left leg as far as possible.
3. Exhale, slowly flex your trunk laterally toward your right side, and try to touch the heel of your left leg with both hands.
4. Hold the stretch and relax.
5. Exhale, round up your upper torso, and return to the starting position.

Stretch # 168

1. Sit upright on the floor with both legs straight.
2. Flex your right knee and place the foot as high as possible on your left thigh with the sole of your foot turned up.
3. Exhale, flex your left knee, and place the foot as high as possible on your right thigh with the sole facing up and without forcing the stretch.
4. Hold the stretch and relax.

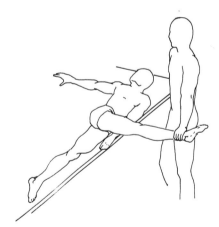

Stretch # 169

1. Lie flat on your back on the edge of a table, with one leg raised and straight and your arm out to the side.
2. Exhale, and slowly lower your raised leg to the opposite side.
3. Your partner stands at your side with one hand grasping your hanging leg.
4. Exhale as you allow your partner to gently push down your hanging leg, while keeping your head and shoulders flat on the table. Communicate with your partner and use great care.
5. Hold the stretch and relax.

Stretch # 170

1. Lie flat on your back with your knees flexed and your hands interlocked beneath your head.
2. Lift your right leg over your left leg and hook your left leg.
3. Your partner is positioned to your side with one hand on your hip to anchor down your body and the other hand on your flexed knee.
4. Exhale as you allow your partner to push your leg to the floor, while keeping your elbows, head, and shoulders flat on the floor. Communicate with your partner and use great care.
5. Hold the stretch and relax.

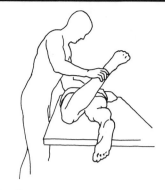

Stretch # 171

1. Lie face down on a table with your body extended.
2. Flex your leg nearest the table edge.
3. Your partner stands at your side with one hand anchoring your body and the other hand grasping your ankle.
4. Exhale as you allow your partner to push your leg toward the opposite side. Communicate with your partner and use great care.
5. Hold the stretch and relax.

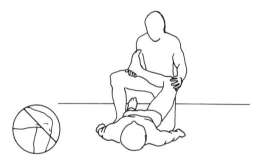

Stretch # 172

1. Lie flat on your back with your body extended.
2. Raise one leg so your thigh is nearly vertical and your knee is flexed.
3. Exhale, and slowly move your foot in toward your body.
4. Your partner is positioned in front of you and to your side, on one knee with the opposite foot on the floor, and holding your knee and ankle of the side to be stretched.
5. Exhale as you allow your partner to slowly move your foot toward your body. Communicate with your partner and use great care.
6. Hold the stretch and relax.

Stretch # 173

1. Stand upright with your right side against a wall.
2. Flex your left knee and raise your foot.
3. Your partner stands in front of you and grasps your leg in a flexed position.
4. Inhale as you allow your partner to slowly push your leg, bending your knee even farther. Communicate with your partner and use great care.
5. Hold the stretch and relax.

External Hip Rotators

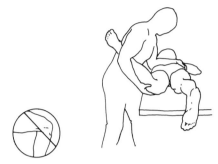

Stretch # 174

1. Lie face down on a table with your body extended.
2. Flex your leg nearest the table edge.
3. Your partner stands at your side with one hand anchoring your body and the other hand grasping the lower leg.
4. Exhale as you allow your partner to pull your leg away from your body. Communicate with your partner and use great care.
5. Hold the stretch and relax.

Stretch # 175

1. Lie flat on your back with your body extended.
2. Raise one leg so the thigh is nearly vertical and the knee is flexed.
3. Exhale, and slowly move your foot away from your body.
4. Your partner is positioned in front of you and to the side, on one knee with the opposite foot on the floor, and holding your knee and ankle of the side to be stretched.
5. Exhale as you allow your partner to slowly move your foot away from your body. Communicate with your partner and use great care.
6. Hold the stretch and relax.

Abdomen and Hip Flexors

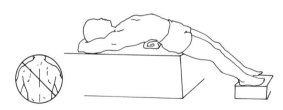

Stretch # 176

1. Lie on a bed with your lower torso hanging over the edge.
2. Hold the stretch and relax.

 This should be avoided by those with lordosis.

Stretch # 177

1. Lie on a bed with your lower torso hanging over the edge.
2. Exhale and lift your left elbow off the surface.
3. Hold the stretch and relax.

 This should be avoided by those with lordosis.

Stretch # 178

1. Lie face down on the floor with your body extended.
2. Place your palms on the floor by your hips with your fingers pointing forward.
3. Exhale, press down on the floor, raise your head and trunk, and arch your back while contracting the gluteals (buttock muscles) to prevent excessive compression on the lower back.
4. Hold the stretch and relax.

Stretch # 179

1. Kneel upright on the floor with legs slightly apart and parallel and with toes pointing backward.
2. Place your palms on your upper hips and buttocks.
3. Exhale, slowly arch your back, contract your buttocks, and push your hips forward.
4. Exhale, continue to arch your back, drop your head backward, open your mouth, and gradually slide your hands onto your heels.
5. Hold the stretch and relax.

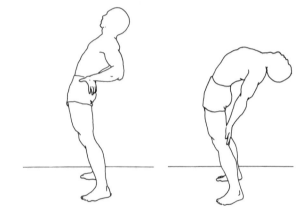

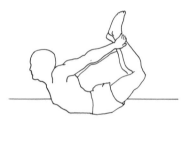

Stretch # 180

1. Stand upright with legs straddled 2 or 3 feet apart and your hands placed on your hips.
2. Exhale, slowly arch your back, contract your buttocks, and push your hips forward.
3. Exhale, continue arching your back, drop your head backward, open your mouth, and gradually slide your hands below your buttocks.
4. Hold the stretch and relax.

Stretch # 181

1. Lie face down on the floor with your body extended.
2. Flex your knees and move your heels toward your hips.
3. Inhale, reach back, and grasp both feet.
4. Inhale, contract the buttocks, and lift your chest and knees off the floor.
5. Hold the stretch and relax.

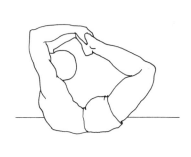

Stretch # 182

1. Lie face down on the floor with your body extended.
2. Flex your knees and move your heels toward your hips.
3. Inhale, reach back, and grasp both feet.
4. Inhale, contract the buttocks, and lift your chest and knees off the floor.
5. Exhale, and pull your feet to your head.
6. Hold the stretch and relax.

Stretch # 183

1. Lie face down on the floor with your body extended.
2. Flex your knees and move your heels toward your hips.
3. Inhale, reach back, and grasp both feet.
4. Inhale, contract the buttocks, and lift your chest and knees off the floor.
5. Exhale, and pull your legs to a vertical position.
6. Hold the stretch and relax.

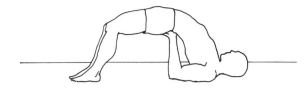

Stretch # 184

1. Lie flat on your back with your body extended.
2. Flex your knees and slide your heels toward your buttocks, keeping them hip-distance apart.
3. Inhale. Keeping your feet flat on the floor, contract your gluteals (buttock muscles), lift your pelvis off the floor, and support your weight with your hands.
4. Hold the stretch and relax.

Stretch # 185

1. Lie flat on your back with your body extended.
2. Flex your knees and slide your heels toward your buttocks, keeping them hip-distance apart.
3. Inhale. Keeping your feet flat on the floor, contract your gluteals, lift your pelvis off the floor, and support your weight with your hands.
4. Exhale, and grasp your ankles.
5. Hold the stretch and relax.

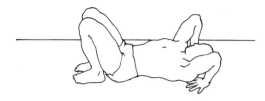

Stretch # 186

1. Lie flat on your back with your heels close to your hips, your hands placed on the floor by your neck (under the shoulders), and your fingers pointing toward your feet.
2. Inhale, raise your trunk, and rest your forehead on the floor.
3. Hold the stretch and relax.

Stretch # 187

1. Lie on your back with your heels close to your hips, your hands placed on the floor by your neck (under the shoulders), and your fingers pointing toward your feet.
2. Inhale, raise your trunk, and rest your forehead on the floor.
3. Exhale, raise one arm at a time, and place your forearms on the floor.
4. Hold the stretch and relax.

Stretch # 188

1. Lie on your back with your heels close to your hips, your hands placed on the floor by your neck (under the shoulders), and your fingers pointing toward your feet.
2. Exhale, extend your arms and legs, and raise your body into a full bridge with your wrists parallel to your shoulders.
3. Hold the stretch and relax.
4. Exhale, and return to the starting position.

Stretch # 189

1. Stand upright with your back about 2 or 3 feet from a wall and with your hands on the wall at about head height.
2. Exhale, and "walk" your hands down the wall. If necessary, use a spotter to provide assistance and support.
3. Hold the stretch and relax.
4. Then walk your hands back up the wall to your starting position.

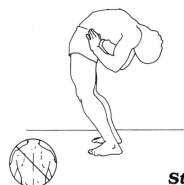

Stretch # 190

1. Stand upright with feet shoulder-width apart and your palms on your hips.
2. Exhale, push your hips forward, and arch your back.
3. Raise your arms overhead while continuing to arch backward, and place your hands on the floor, ending up in a bridge position with your arms straight and no more than shoulder-width apart. If necessary, use a spotter for assistance and support.
4. Hold the stretch and relax.
5. Flex your arms and lower yourself onto your shoulders.

Stretch # 191

1. Stand upright with the body extended, one leg raised to a 45-degree angle, hips squared, arms straight and vertical, and elbows by the ears.
2. Exhale, tilt the head backward between the arms, and arch backward as your eyes follow the hands.
3. When the hands contact the mat, the arms *must* be straight and shoulder-width apart. If necessary, use a spotter for assistance and support.
4. Initiate a strong extension of the ankle of the supporting foot and the shoulders when your weight transfers from the supporting foot to the hands and when shoulders are directly over the hands.
5. As the trailing leg leaves the floor, you will pass through a split-position handstand, with your head between your arms and down.
6. When the lead foot contacts the floor, the hands must push off the floor to return the body to an erect position.

Stretch # 192

1. Stand upright with the body extended, one leg raised to a 45-degree angle, hips squared, arms straight and vertical, and elbows by the ears.
2. Step forward onto the lead leg, lower your upper torso, and place your hands on the floor shoulder-width apart.
3. Immediately push off with the supporting leg and arms.
4. Pass through a split-position handstand with your body extended and head between your arms.
5. Continue to arch over, and attempt to place your supporting leg close to your hands. If necessary, use a spotter for assistance and support.
6. Then push off with your hands, thrust your hips forward, straighten your supporting leg, and return to an upright position.

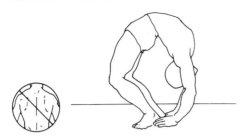

Stretch # 193

1. Lie flat on your back with your heels close to your hips, your hands placed on the floor by your neck (under the shoulders), and your fingers pointing toward your feet.
2. Exhale, extend your arms and legs, and raise your body into a full bridge.
3. Exhale, and slowly close the distance between your hands and your feet until they are touching.
4. Hold the stretch and relax.
5. Separate your hands and feet, flex your arms, and lower yourself down onto your shoulders.

■ Obviously, this skill requires exceptional suppleness. However, its value is doubtful for even most elite athletes.

Stretch # 194

1. Lie flat on your back with your body extended.
2. Flex your knees, and slide your heels toward your buttocks, keeping them hip-distance apart.
3. Exhale, grasp your ankles, contract your gluteals, and lift your pelvis off the floor while keeping your feet and shoulders flat on the floor.
4. Your partner sits on the floor with one leg between your straddled legs, the foot resting against the middle of your upper back, and grasping your wrists.
5. Exhale as you allow your partner to pull on your arms and push evenly into both sides of your lower back. Communicate with your partner and use great care.
6. Hold the stretch and relax.

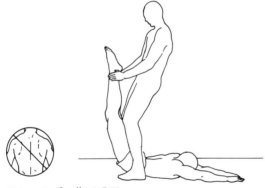

Stretch # 195

1. Lie face down on the floor with your body extended and your arms parallel and stretched forward.
2. Your partner straddles your hips, facing your feet.
3. Your partner bends at the hips and knees, reaches down, and grasps your legs at about the lower legs or ankles.
4. Exhale, and contract your gluteals to prevent compression of your lower back as you allow your partner to slowly lift your thighs off the floor. Communicate with your partner and use great care.
5. Hold the stretch and relax.

Stretch # 196

1. Lie face down on the floor with your body extended and your arms parallel and stretched forward.
2. Your partner straddles your hips, facing your head.
3. Your partner bends at the hips and knees, reaches down, and grasps your shoulders.
4. Exhale, and contract your gluteals to prevent compression of your lower back as you allow your partner to lift your upper torso off the floor.
5. Hold the stretch and relax.

BACK AND TRUNK

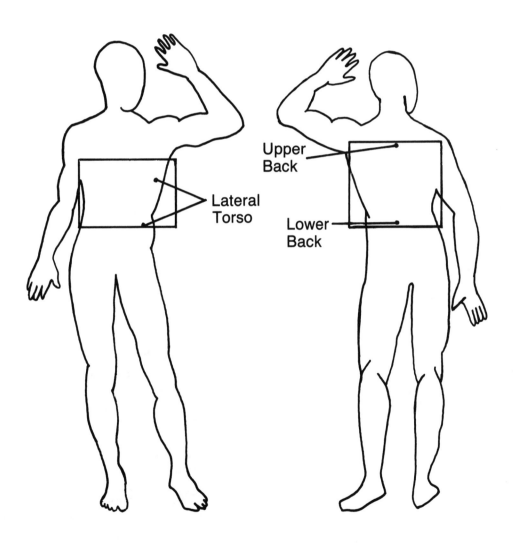

Upper
Back

Lateral
Torso

Lower
Back

Lower Back

Stretch # 197

1. Kneel on all fours with your toes facing backward.
2. Inhale, contract your abdominals, and round your back.
3. Exhale, relax your abdominals, and return to the "flat back" position.

Stretch # 198

1. Sit upright in a chair with your legs straddled.
2. Exhale, extend your upper torso, bend at the waist, and slowly lower your stomach between your thighs.
3. Hold the stretch and relax.

Stretch # 199

1. Sit upright on a bed or bench with your knees flexed.
2. Exhale, extend your upper torso, bend at the waist, and slowly lower your stomach onto your thighs.
3. Exhale, and slowly extend your legs.
4. Hold the stretch and relax.

Stretch # 200

1. Lie flat on your back with your body extended.
2. Flex your knees, and slide your feet toward your buttocks.
3. Grasp behind your thighs to prevent hyperextension of the knees.
4. Exhale, pull your knees toward your chest and shoulders, and elevate your hips off the floor.
5. Hold the stretch and relax.
6. Exhale, and extend your legs slowly, one at a time, to prevent possible pain or spasm.

Stretch # 201

1. Lie flat on your back with your body extended.
2. Flex your knees, and slide your feet toward your buttocks.
3. Your partner is positioned to your side with one hand under your hamstrings and the other grasping your heels.
4. Exhale as you allow your partner to bring your thighs closer to your chest.
5. Hold the stretch and relax.
6. Exhale, and extend your legs slowly, one at a time, to prevent possible pain or spasm.

Stretch # 202

1. Lie flat on your back with your arms by your hips, palms down.
2. Inhale, push down on the floor with your palms, raise your legs up in a squat position so the knees almost rest on your forehead, and bring your hands up to support your back.
3. Hold the stretch and relax.

▼ Use this controversial stretch with care.

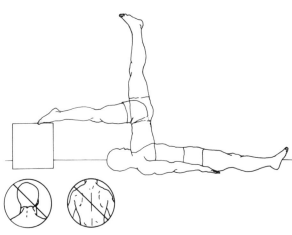

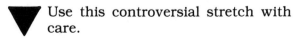

Stretch # 203

1. Lie flat on your back with your arms by your hips, palms down.
2. Inhale, push down on the floor with your palms, and raise your legs to a vertical position.
3. Exhale, keep your legs straight, and lower your feet onto a chair.
4. Hold the stretch and relax.

▼ Use this controversial stretch with care.

Stretch # 204

1. Lie flat on your back with your arms by your hips, palms down.
2. Inhale, push down on the floor with your palms, raise your legs to a vertical position, and support your body with your hands placed on your lower back.
3. Exhale, split your legs, and lower one to the floor while the other remains vertical. If you lack sufficient flexibility, just lower your leg to a horizontal position.
4. Hold the stretch and relax.

▼ Use this controversial stretch with care.

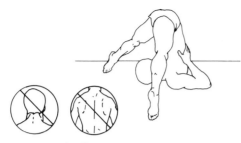

Stretch # 205

1. Lie flat on your back with your arms by your hips, palms down.
2. Inhale, push down on the floor with your palms, raise your legs to a vertical position, and support your body with your hands placed on your lower back.
3. Exhale, keep your legs straight and straddled, and lower your feet to the floor.
4. Hold the stretch and relax.

▼ Use this controversial stretch with care.

Stretch # 206

1. Lie flat on your back with your arms by your hips, palms down.
2. Inhale, push down on the floor with your palms, raise your legs to a vertical position, and support your body with your hands placed on your lower back.
3. Exhale, keep your legs straight and together, and lower your feet to the floor.
4. Hold the stretch and relax.

▼ Use this controversial stretch with care.

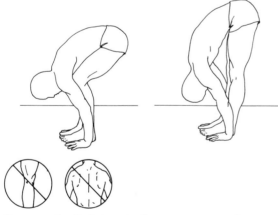

Stretch # 207 (Also Hamstrings)

1. Assume a squat position with your hands resting on the floor.
2. Exhale, and slowly extend your knees. Stop when you feel excess tension.
3. Hold the stretch and relax.

■ The stretches that follow present a greater degree of risk of injury. For the typical layperson, this exercise offers a safer alternative that accomplishes the same purpose.

Stretch # 208 (Also Hamstrings)

1. Stand upright with your legs straight and hands by your sides.
2. Exhale, flex forward at the waist, slide your hands down to your knees, and keep your back flat.
3. Hold the stretch and relax.
4. Exhale, and bend the knees or round the upper torso up rather than lifting with an arched back when returning to the upright position.

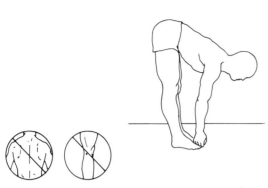

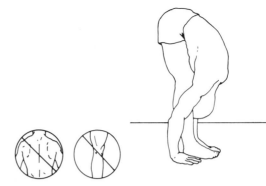

Stretch # 209 (Also Hamstrings)

1. Stand upright with your legs straight and hands by your sides.
2. Exhale, flex forward at the waist, slide your hands down to your knees, and keep your back flat.
3. Exhale, and continue lowering your hands until they touch your toes.
4. Hold the stretch and relax.
5. Exhale, and bend the knees or round the upper torso up rather than lifting with an arched back when returning to the upright position.

Stretch # 210 (Also Hamstrings)

1. Stand upright with your legs straight and hands by your sides.
2. Exhale, flex forward at the waist, slide your hands down your knees, and keep your back flat.
3. Exhale, and continue lowering your hands until they are flat on the floor and your upper torso touches your thighs.
4. Hold the stretch and relax.
5. Exhale, and bend the knees or round the upper torso up rather than lifting with an arched back when returning to the upright position.

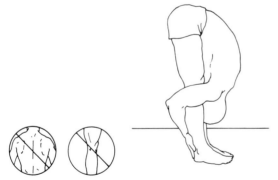

Stretch # 211 (Also Hamstrings)

1. Stand upright with your legs straight and hands by your sides.
2. Exhale, flex forward at the waist, slide your hands down your knees, and keep your back flat.
3. Exhale, slide your hands behind your calves, and pull your upper torso onto your thighs.
4. Hold the stretch and relax.
5. Exhale, and bend the knees or round the upper torso up rather than lifting with an arched back when returning to the upright position.

Stretch # 212

1. Lie on a table face down.
2. Exhale, and slide forward until your upper torso hangs over the edge from your waist.
3. Your partner stands at your side, anchoring your body.
4. Hold the stretch and relax.

 Inversion stretches should be avoided by those with glaucoma, hypertension, weakness in blood vessels, and spinal instability.

Stretch # 213

1. Hang from a chin-up bar with a forward grip.
2. Pull down on the bar, flex your legs, and raise them between your hands so the backs of your knees rest on the bar. Use a spotter for assistance.
3. Release the bar with your hands, and hang from the back of your knees.
4. Hold the stretch and relax.

▼ Inversion stretches should be avoided by those with glaucoma, hypertension, weakness in blood vessels, and spinal instability.

Stretch # 214

1. Put on a pair of inversion boots.
2. Hang from a chin-up bar with a forward grip.
3. Pull down on the bar, flex your knees, and raise them between your hands so you can hook the boots to the bar.
4. Release the bar and hang from the boots.
5. Hold the stretch and relax.

▼ Inversion stretches should be avoided by those with glaucoma, hypertension, weakness in blood vessels, and spinal instability.

■ There are many different types of inversion devices on the market. Some are safer to use than others. Regardless of the brand or model, receive proper instruction and supervision before using.

Lateral Trunk

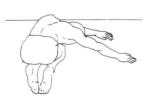

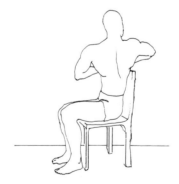

Stretch # 215

1. Kneel on all fours.
2. Straighten your arms, reach forward as far as possible, and lower your chest to the floor.
3. Exhale, slightly twist your upper torso, and press down with palms and forearms on the floor.
4. Hold the stretch and relax.

Stretch # 216

1. Sit upright in a chair.
2. Exhale, turn to your right, and place your hands on the back of the chair.
3. Exhale, keep your feet flat on the floor and buttocks flat on the seat, push your right hip forward, and press your right elbow into your body.
4. Hold the stretch and relax.

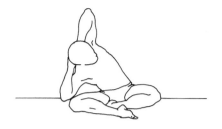

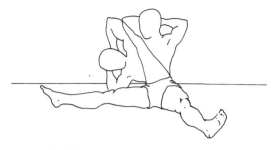

Stretch # 217

1. Sit upright on the floor with your legs crossed.
2. Interlock your hands behind your head with the elbows lifted.
3. Exhale, bring your right elbow to your right knee, and keep your left shoulder and elbow back.
4. Hold the stretch and relax.

Stretch # 218

1. Sit upright on the floor with your legs straight and straddled.
2. Interlock your hands behind your head with your elbows lifted.
3. Exhale, and bend your upper torso to the side, attempting to touch your right elbow to the floor outside your right thigh while keeping your left shoulder and elbow back.
4. Hold the stretch and relax.

Stretch # 219

1. Kneel upright on the floor.
2. Extend your right leg out to the side, keeping it in line with your left knee, and raise your arms sideways.
3. Exhale, bend from the hips to the right, lower your right hand onto your right foot, and extend your left arm over your left ear.
4. Hold the stretch and relax.

Stretch # 220

1. Sit upright on the floor with your legs straight and straddled.
2. Lean backward, and place your hands behind your hips and on the floor for support.
3. Exhale, support yourself on your heel(s), swing your left arm overhead and to the right, and lift your hips off the floor.
4. Hold the stretch and relax.

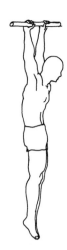

Stretch # 221

1. Stand upright with feet slightly apart and hands interlocking overhead.
2. Exhale, drop one ear toward your shoulder, and slowly lower your arms sideways.
3. Hold the stretch and relax.

Stretch # 222

1. Hang from a chin-up bar with your arms straight, hands almost touching, and your body in a hollow position.
2. Exhale, place your chin on your chest, and sink in your shoulders.
3. Hold the stretch and relax.

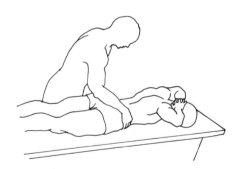

Stretch # 223

1. Hang from a chin-up bar with your arms straight.
2. Release one hand at a time, and regrasp the bar in an L-grip (the back of the hand faces up and the thumb grasps under the bar).
3. Hold the stretch and relax.

Stretch # 224

1. Lie face down on a table with your hands interlocked behind your head.
2. Your partner stands at your side with his or her hands anchoring your pelvis.
3. Exhale as you attempt to twist your upper torso sideways.
4. Hold the stretch and relax.

Stretch # 225

1. Lie face down on a table and hold the sides for stability.
2. Your partner stands at your side and grasps underneath your thighs.
3. Exhale as you allow your partner to lift and pull your lower torso laterally.
4. Hold the stretch and relax.

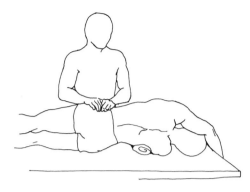

Stretch # 226

1. Lie sideways on a table with your top arm stretched overhead. Use a folded towel to reduce discomfort on your side.
2. Your partner stands at your side and anchors down your hip.
3. Hold the stretch and relax.

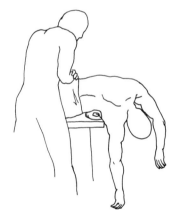

Stretch # 227

1. Lie over the edge of a table with both arms hanging downward. Use a folded towel to reduce discomfort on your side.
2. Your partner stands at your side and anchors down your hips.
3. Hold the stretch and relax.

Stretch # 228

1. Kneel upright on the floor.
2. Extend your right leg out to the side, keeping it in line with your left knee, and raise your arm sideways.
3. Your partner stands behind you with one hand anchoring your hip and the other hand grasping your extended arm.
4. Exhale as you allow your partner to stretch your side. Communicate with your partner and use great care.
5. Hold the stretch and relax.

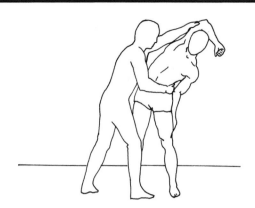

Stretch # 229

1. Stand upright with your feet slightly apart, one arm by your side, and your other arm flexed overhead.
2. Your partner stands at your side with one hand on your hip and the other holding your raised arm on or below your elbow.
3. Exhale, and bend your trunk to one side with no forward or backward flexing.
4. Exhale as you allow your partner to gently push your trunk farther to one side. Communicate with your partner and use great care.
5. Hold the stretch and relax.

Stretch # 230

1. Lie face down on a table with your upper torso extended over the edge, grasping with both hands a stretching stick that rests across your shoulders.
2. Exhale as you twist your upper torso as high as possible.
3. Hold the stretch and relax.
4. Exhale, and return to the starting position.

Stretch # 231

1. Stand upright with your feet parallel and shoulder-width apart, one arm flexed behind your head, and your other hand holding a light dumbbell at your side.
2. Exhale, maintain your body in a lateral plane, and bend sideways as far as possible.
3. Hold the stretch and relax.
4. Exhale, and return to the starting position.

Stretch # 232

1. Stand upright with your feet parallel and shoulder-width apart and knees slightly flexed, a light barbell resting across your shoulders.
2. Exhale, and slowly turn your trunk as far as possible to one side.
3. Hold the stretch and relax.
4. Exhale, and return to the starting position.

Upper Back

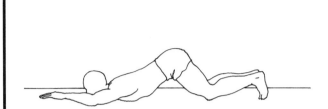

Stretch # 233

1. Kneel on all fours.
2. Extend your arms forward, and lower your chest toward the floor.
3. Exhale, extend your shoulders, and press down on the floor with your arms to produce an arch in your back.
4. Hold the stretch and relax.

Stretch # 234

1. Stand upright with your feet together, about 3 feet from a supporting surface at approximately waist to shoulder height, and your arms overhead.
2. Exhale. Keeping your arms and legs straight, flex at the waist, flatten your back, and grasp the supporting surface with both hands.
3. Exhale, extend your shoulders, and press down on the supporting surface to produce an arch in your back.
4. Hold the stretch and relax.

Stretch # 235

1. Sit upright with knees straddled, facing a wall about an arm's length away.
2. Raise your arms with your elbows straight, lean forward, and place your arms and hands against the wall shoulder-width apart with your fingers pointing upward.
3. Exhale, extend your shoulders, press down against the wall, open your chest, and produce an arch in your back.

4. Your partner is positioned directly behind you with hands placed on the upper portion of your shoulder blades.
5. Exhale as you allow your partner to gently push down and away from your head. Communicate with your partner and use great care.
6. Hold the stretch and relax.

Rhomboids

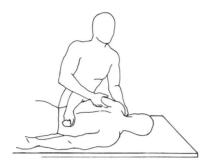

Stretch # 236

1. Lie flat on your stomach with your head turned to the left and your left arm flexed and resting on your lower back.
2. Your partner is positioned to your side with his or her left hand grasping the top front of your shoulder.
3. Exhale as you allow your partner to lift your front shoulder and scapula.
4. The partner places his or her hand under your scapula and gently lifts it upward.
5. Hold the stretch and relax.

NECK AND CHEST

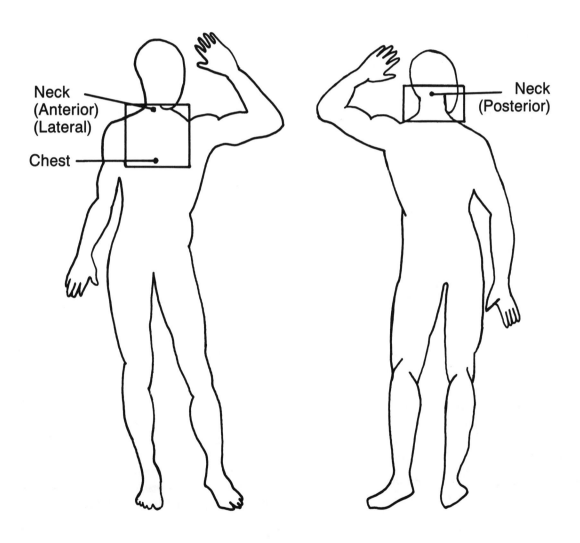

Neck
(Anterior)
(Lateral)

Chest

Neck
(Posterior)

Posterior Neck

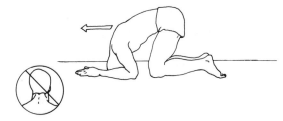

Stretch # 237

1. Lie flat on the floor with both knees flexed.
2. Interlock your hands on the back of your head near the crown.
3. Exhale, and pull your head off the floor and onto your chest. Keep your shoulder blades flat on the floor.
4. Hold the stretch and relax.

Stretch # 238

1. Stand or sit upright.
2. Interlock your hands on the back of your head near the crown.
3. Exhale, pull down on your head, and allow your chin to rest on your chest. Keep your shoulders depressed during the stretch.
4. Hold the stretch and relax.

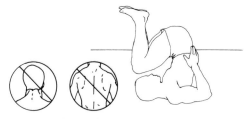

Stretch # 239

1. Kneel on all fours.
2. Flex your arms, and place the crown of your head on the floor.
3. Exhale, roll your head forward, and bring your chin to your chest.
4. Hold the stretch and relax.

■ This is an essential stretch for wrestlers.

Stretch # 240

1. Lie flat on your back with your arms by your hips, palms down.
2. Exhale, push down on the floor with your palms, raise your legs and buttocks off the floor, and rest your knees on your forehead.
3. Bend your elbows, and place your hands on your lower back for support.
4. Hold the stretch and relax.

 This is considered a controversial stretch.

Stretch # 241

1. Lie flat on your back with your hands by your hips, palms down.
2. Exhale, push down on the floor with your palms, raise your legs and buttocks off the floor, and extend your legs vertically.
3. Bend your elbows, and place your hands on your lower back for support.
4. Hold the stretch and relax.

▼ This is considered a controversial stretch.

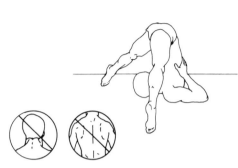

Stretch # 242

1. Lie flat on your back with your hands by your hips, palms down.
2. Exhale, push down on the floor with your palms, raise your legs and buttocks off the floor, and extend your legs vertically.
3. Bend the elbows and place your hands on your lower back for support.
4. Exhale, keep your legs straight and straddled, and lower your feet to the floor.
5. Hold the stretch and relax.

▼ This is considered a controversial stretch.

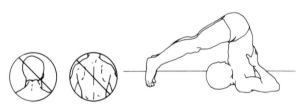

Stretch # 243

1. Lie flat on your back with your hands by your hips, palms down.
2. Exhale, push down on the floor with your palms, and raise your legs to a vertical position.
3. Exhale, keep your legs straight and together, lower your feet to the floor, and bring your hands up to support your back.
4. Hold the stretch and relax.

▼ This is considered a controversial stretch.

Stretch # 244

1. Lie flat on your back with your hands by your hips, palms down.
2. Exhale, push down on the floor with your palms, raise your legs and buttocks off the floor, and rest your knees on your forehead.
3. Exhale, bring your chin onto your chest, and flex the knees to the floor on both sides at your ears.
4. Exhale, lower your arms to the floor, and interlock your hands.
5. Hold the stretch and relax.

▼ This is considered a controversial stretch.

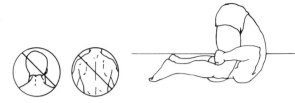

Stretch # 245

1. Lie flat on your back with your hands by your hips, palms down.
2. Exhale, push down on the floor with your palms, raise your legs and buttocks off the floor, and rest your knees on your forehead.
3. Exhale, bring your chin onto your chest, and flex the knees to the floor on both sides at your ears.
4. Exhale, put your hands behind your legs, and pull your thighs to your chest.
5. Hold the stretch and relax.

▼ This is considered a controversial stretch.

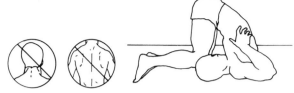

Stretch # 246

1. Lie flat on your back with your hands by your hips, palms down,
2. Exhale, push down on the floor with your palms, raise your legs and buttocks off the floor, and rest your knees on your forehead.
3. Exhale, lower your knees to the left side of your head, and bring your hands up to support your back.
4. Hold the stretch and relax.

▼ This is considered a controversial stretch.

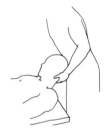

Stretch # 247

1. Lie flat on the floor, or on a table with your head hanging over the edge.
2. Your partner is positioned behind your head with both hands holding your head.
3. Exhale as you allow your partner to gently lift your head and bring it to your chest. Communicate with your partner and use great care.
4. Hold the stretch and relax.

Stretch # 248

1. Lie flat on your back with your hands by your hips, palms down.
2. Exhale, push down on the floor with your palms, raise your legs and buttocks off the floor, and rest your knees on your forehead.
3. Exhale, bring your chin onto your chest, and place your shins flat on the floor with your knees touching your shoulders.
4. Exhale, lower your arms to the floor, and interlock your hands.
5. Your partner is positioned facing your back, kneeling upright on the floor, legs straddling your arms, and one hand anchoring your arms while the other is on your lower back.
6. Exhale as you allow your partner to gently push your pelvis forward.

▼ This is potentially one of the most dangerous stretches in this book. It should be done with *extreme* discretion!

Lateral Neck

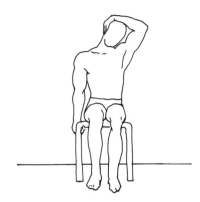

Stretch # 249

1. Sit or stand upright.
2. Place your left hand on the upper right side of your head.
3. Exhale, and slowly pull the left side of your head onto your left shoulder (lateral flexion).
4. Hold the stretch and relax.

Stretch # 250

1. Sit or stand upright with your left arm flexed behind your back.
2. Grasp the elbow from behind with the opposite hand.
3. Exhale, pull your elbow across the midline of your back, and lower your ear to the right shoulder. It is essential to keep your left shoulder stabilized.
4. Hold the stretch and relax.

Anterior Neck

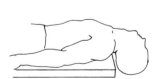

Stretch # 251

1. Lie flat on a table with your head hanging over the edge.
2. Hold the stretch and relax.

Stretch # 252

1. Sit or stand upright and carefully lean your head back.
2. Place your hands on your forehead.
3. Exhale and pull your head backward.
4. Hold the stretch and relax.

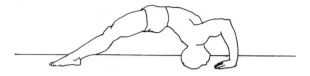

Stretch # 253

1. Lie flat on your back with your heels close to your hips, your hands placed on the floor by your neck (under the shoulders), and your fingers pointing toward your feet.
2. Exhale, raise your trunk, and rest your forehead on the floor.
3. Exhale, and roll your head backward.
4. Hold the stretch and relax.

■ This is an essential stretch for wrestlers.

Pectorals

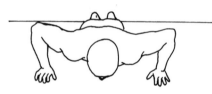

Stretch # 254

1. Lie flat on a table with your legs flexed, upper trunk hanging over the edge, and hands interlocked behind your head.
2. Exhale, and lower your head and shoulders toward the floor.
3. Hold the stretch and relax.

■ Keep your neck extended and elbows spread widely apart. Also, if necessary have a partner anchor your feet.

Stretch # 255

1. Assume a front prone support (push-up) position with your arms as wide as possible.
2. Exhale, and slowly lower your chest almost to the floor.
3. Hold the stretch and relax.
4. Exhale and return to the starting position.

■ This requires adequate strength to support yourself.

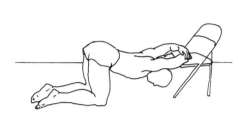

Stretch # 256

1. Sit upright with hands interlocked behind your head and the top of the chair at midchest level.
2. Exhale, lean your upper torso backward, and pull your arms backward.
3. Hold the stretch and relax.

Stretch # 257

1. Kneel on the floor facing a barre or chair at knee height.
2. Flex your arms, and rest your interlocked forearms on top of the barre or chair, with your head dropping beneath the supporting surface.
3. Exhale, and let your head and chest sink to the floor.
4. Hold the stretch and relax.

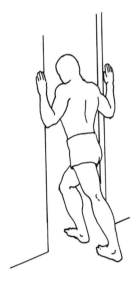

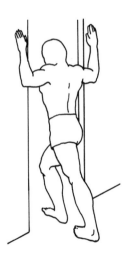

Stretch # 258

1. Stand upright facing a corner or open doorway.
2. Raise your arms in a reverse "T" (elbows below your shoulders) to stretch the collarbone section of your pectoral muscles bilaterally.
3. Exhale, and lean your entire body forward.
4. Hold the stretch and relax.

Stretch # 259

1. Stand upright facing a corner or open doorway.
2. Raise your arms to form the letter "T" (elbows level with your shoulders) to stretch the breastbone section of the pectoral muscles bilaterally.
3. Exhale, and lean your entire body forward.
4. Hold the stretch and relax.

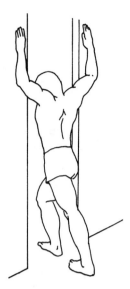

Stretch # 260

1. Stand upright facing a corner or open doorway.
2. Raise your arms to form the letter "V" (elbows raised above your shoulders) to stretch the rib section of the pectoral muscles bilaterally.
3. Exhale, and lean your entire body forward.
4. Hold the stretch and relax.

Stretch # 261

1. Sit upright with both arms flexed and your hands interlocked behind your head.
2. Your partner stands behind you and grasps both elbows.
3. Exhale as you allow your partner to gently pull your elbows backward toward each other. Communicate with your partner and use great care.
4. Hold the stretch and relax.

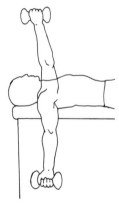

Stretch # 262

1. Lie on a bench with your legs flexed and your feet resting on its surface.
2. Hold two light dumbbells directly over your chest, with your arms flexed and your knuckles facing out.
3. Inhale. Keeping your arms flexed, lower your dumbbells sideways, keeping your elbows as close to the floor as possible.
4. Hold the stretch and relax.

5. Exhale, and return to the starting position by bringing the dumbbells back up in an arc.

 If you vary this stretch by executing these "flys" with straight arms, perform them properly and use very light weights. This exercise can apply extreme tension to the elbow and shoulder joints.

SHOULDERS

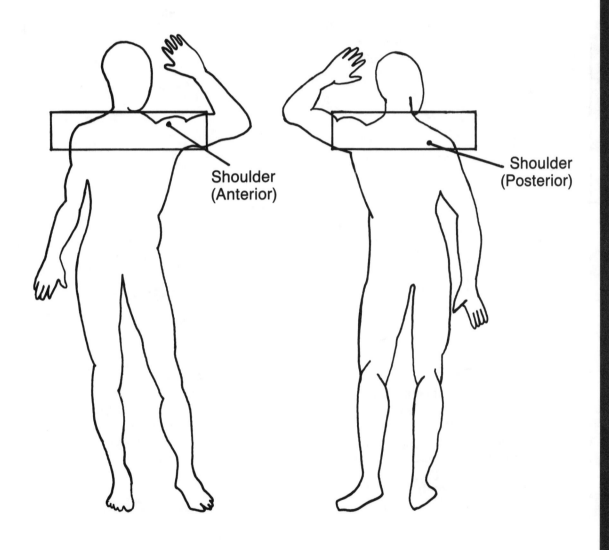

Shoulder
(Anterior)

Shoulder
(Posterior)

Anterior Shoulder

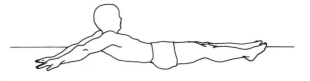

Stretch # 263

1. Sit upright on the floor with your hands about 1 foot behind your hips, your fingers pointing away from your body, and your legs extended forward.
2. Inhale, lift your buttocks, raise your trunk off the floor, and open your chest as wide as possible.
3. Hold the stretch and relax.

Stretch # 264

1. Sit upright on the floor with your hands about 1 foot behind your hips, your fingers pointing away from your body, palms down, and your legs extended forward.
2. Exhale, slide your buttocks forward, and lean backward as far as possible.
3. Hold the stretch and relax.

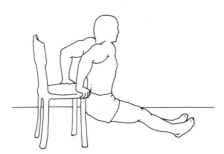

Stretch # 265

1. Stand upright, with your hands behind your hips at about shoulder height, resting on a wall, and your fingers pointing upward.
2. Exhale, and flex your legs to lower your shoulders.
3. Hold the stretch and relax.

Stretch # 266

1. Brace yourself on a stable and sturdy chair with your body extended, hips forward, and arms straight.
2. Exhale, flex your arms, and lower your buttocks toward the floor.
3. Hold the stretch and relax.

Stretch # 267

1. Hang from a pair of still rings.
2. Inhale, and raise your body to an inverted hang.
3. Exhale, and slowly lower your legs to the floor (Skin the Cat). Try to sink as low as possible in the shoulders.
4. Hold the stretch and relax.

Stretch # 268

1. Sit upright on the floor, with your hands about 1 foot behind your hips, your fingers pointing away from your body, palms down, and your legs extended forward.
2. Exhale, slide your buttocks forward, and lean backward as far as possible.
3. Your partner kneels directly behind you, holding both wrists.
4. Exhale as you allow your partner to pull your arms backward, upward, and crisscross. Communicate with your partner and use great care.
5. Hold the stretch and relax.

Stretch # 269

1. Sit upright, or kneel on the floor, with your arms raised horizontally behind your back.
2. Your partner is positioned directly behind you, holding both your wrists.

3. Exhale as you allow your partner to pull your arms backward, upward, and crisscross. Communicate with your partner and use great care.
4. Hold the stretch and relax.

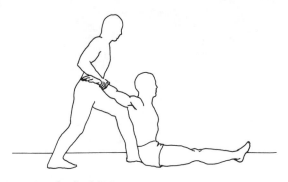

Stretch # 270

1. Sit upright, or kneel on the floor, with your arms raised above the horizontal behind your back.
2. Exhale as you allow your partner to pull your arms backward, upward, and crisscross. Communicate with your partner and use great care.
3. Hold the stretch and relax.

Lateral Shoulder

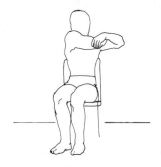

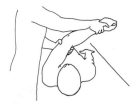

Stretch # 271

1. Sit, or stand upright, with one arm raised to shoulder height.
2. Flex your arm across to the opposite shoulder.
3. Grasp your raised elbow with the opposite hand.
4. Exhale, and pull your elbow backward.
5. Hold the stretch and relax.

Stretch # 272

1. Lie on a table with one arm vertically raised.
2. Your partner stands at your side with one hand grasping your elbow and the other your wrist.
3. Exhale as you allow your partner to gently push your extended arm across your chest. Communicate with your partner and use care.
4. Hold the stretch and relax.

Internal Rotators

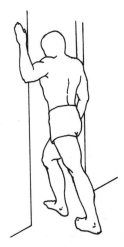

Stretch # 273

1. Sit upright with your side next to a table.
2. Rest your forearm along the table edge with your elbow flexed.
3. Exhale, bend forward from the waist, and lower your head and shoulder to table level.
4. Hold the stretch and relax.

Stretch # 274

1. Stand upright facing the edge of a door frame.
2. Raise your arm, flex your elbow, and place your hand on the frame.
3. Exhale, and turn away from your fixed arm as it remains against your side.
4. Hold the stretch and relax.

Stretch # 275

1. Sit or stand upright.
2. Flex your right arm, and raise the elbow to chest height.
3. Flex and raise your left arm so its elbow can support your right elbow.
4. Intertwine your forearms so that your left hand grasps your right wrist.
5. Exhale, and pull your wrist outward and downward.
6. Hold the stretch and relax.

Stretch # 276

1. Lie flat on your back on a table.
2. Flex your arm with your elbow resting over the edge.
3. Your partner stands at your side with one hand anchoring your elbow and the other grasping your wrist.
4. Exhale as you allow your partner to gently push downward on your wrist. Communicate with your partner and use great care.
5. Hold the stretch and relax.

Stretch # 277

1. Stand upright with your right arm raised to shoulder height and flexed to a right angle.
2. Your partner stands in front of you and to your side, grasping your right wrist with his or her left hand and supporting your right elbow with his or her right hand.
3. Exhale as you allow your partner to gently push your wrist backward and downward. Communicate with your partner and use great care.
4. Hold the stretch and relax.

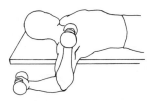

Stretch # 278

1. Lie flat on a bench or table with your arm resting over the edge and your elbow flexed to a 90-degree angle while holding a light dumbbell.
2. Inhale, and slowly lower the weight downward and parallel to your head.
3. Hold the stretch and relax.
4. Exhale, and return to the starting position.

▼ This stretch should be avoided by anyone who has recently suffered an anterior shoulder dislocation. The stretch should be done only after the injury has healed, and then with a partner providing support under the wrist.

External Rotators

Stretch # 279

1. Sit or stand upright with one arm flexed behind your back.
2. Grasp the elbow from behind with the opposite hand.
3. Exhale, and pull your elbow across the midline of your back. (Grasp the wrist if you are unable to reach your elbow.)
4. Hold the stretch and relax.

Stretch # 280

1. Sit or stand upright.
2. Place your palms together behind your back with your fingers pointing downward.
3. Exhale, rotate your wrists so that your fingers are pointing toward your head, and then draw your elbows back.
4. Hold the stretch and relax.

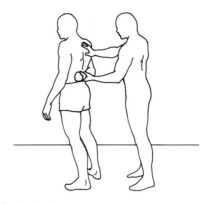

Stretch # 281

1. Sit or kneel upright with your palms together behind your back and your fingers pointing downward.
2. Exhale, and rotate your wrists so that your fingers are pointing toward your head.
3. Your partner is positioned directly behind you, grasping both elbows.
4. Exhale as you allow your partner to gently pull your elbows backward. Communicate with your partner and use great care.
5. Hold the stretch and relax.

Stretch # 282

1. Stand upright with one arm behind your back and the thumb up.
2. Reach your hand as high as possible to the opposite shoulder.
3. Your partner stands directly behind you with one hand anchored against your scapula and the other hand grasping your wrist.
4. Inhale as your partner gently pulls your hand away from your back. Communicate with your partner and use great care.
5. Hold the stretch and relax.

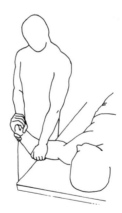

Stretch # 283

1. Lie flat on your back on a table.
2. Flex your arm, and rest your elbow over the edge.
3. Your partner stands at your side with one hand anchoring your elbow and the other grasping your wrist.
4. Exhale as you allow your partner to push your hand forward and downward toward your feet. Communicate with your partner and use great care.
5. Hold the stretch and relax.

Internal and External Rotators

Stretch # 284

1. Stand upright, with your feet straddled; grasp either a pole or a towel behind your hips with a reverse grip (your fingers facing upward and the thumb around the pole or towel).
2. Inhale, and slowly raise your arms overhead, keeping them straight until they rotate forward in the shoulder joint and end in an L-grip.
3. Inhale, then reverse the direction. (The wider the hand placement, the easier the dislocation. Remember, the arms must be kept straight and symmetrical—no twisting to the side.)

Stretch # 285

1. Stand upright with your feet straddled; grasp either a pole or a towel in front of your hips with an overgrip (regular grip).
2. Inhale, slowly raise your arms overhead, keeping them straight until they rotate in the shoulder joint and end up behind your hips.
3. Inhale, then reverse the direction. (The wider the hand placement, the easier the inlocating action. Remember, the arms must be kept straight and symmetrical—no twisting to the side.)

Shoulder Flexors

Stretch # 286

1. Sit or stand upright.
2. Cross one wrist over the other, and interlock your hands.
3. Inhale, straighten your arms, and extend your arms behind your head. Your elbows should be behind your ears.
4. Hold the stretch and relax.

Stretch # 287

1. Lie flat on your back, with your heels close to your hips, your hands placed on the floor by your neck (under the shoulders), and your fingers pointing toward your feet.
2. Exhale, extend your arms and legs, and raise your body into a full bridge.
3. Exhale, and press your shoulders past your wrists (vertical).
4. Hold the stretch and relax.

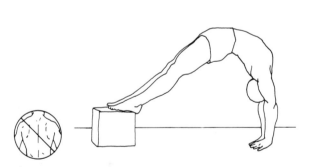

Stretch # 288

1. Lie flat on your back with your feet resting on a bench, your hands placed on the floor by your neck (under the shoulders), and your fingers pointing in the direction of your feet. (Be sure the bench is stable and sturdy.)
2. Inhale, and raise your trunk off the floor into a full bridge.
3. Exhale, and press your shoulders past your wrists (vertical).
4. Hold the stretch and relax.

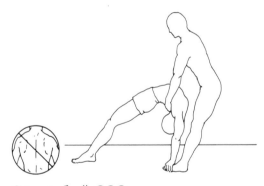

Stretch # 289

1. Lie flat on your back, with your heels close to your hips and your hands grasping the ankles of your partner, who stands straddling your head.
2. Inhale, extend your arms and legs, and raise your body into a full bridge.
3. Your partner reaches under and interlocks his or her hands beneath your shoulders.
4. Inhale as your partner gently lifts you upward. Communicate with your partner and use great care.
5. Hold the stretch and relax.

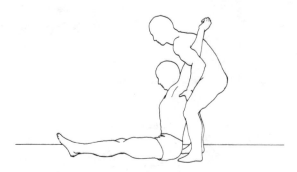

Stretch # 290

1. Sit upright on the floor, with your legs straight and your arms parallel and overhead.
2. Your partner sits on the floor, back-to-back with you in the same position, grasping your wrists.
3. Exhale as you allow your partner to lean forward, pull your wrists, and lift your trunk off the floor. Communicate with your partner and use great care.
4. Hold the stretch and relax.

Stretch # 291

1. Sit upright on the floor, with your legs straight and your arms parallel and overhead.
2. Your partner stands directly behind you with his or her knees braced against your spine.
3. Your partner reaches around your arms, hooks your elbows in his or her armpits, and places his or her hands on your upper shoulder blades.
4. Exhale as you allow your partner to gently push your shoulder blades forward and pull your arms backward. Communicate with your partner and use great care.
5. Hold the stretch and relax.

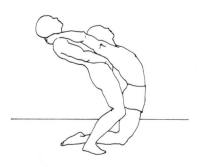

Stretch # 292

1. Kneel upright on the floor with your arms parallel, overhead, and touching your ears.
2. Your partner straddles your legs from behind and grasps the top side of your shoulder blades.
3. Grasp your partner around the neck, interlocking your hands.
4. Inhale as your partner lifts up and leans backward. Communicate with your partner and use great care.
5. Hold the stretch and relax.

Stretch # 293

1. Stand upright, with your feet together and your arms parallel, overhead, and touching your ears.
2. Your partner stands back-to-back with you, with knees flexed and buttocks beneath you.
3. Your partner reaches upward and grasps your arms at or below the elbow.
4. Exhale as your partner leans forward, slightly straightens his or her legs, and lifts you off the floor.
5. Hold the stretch and relax.

Stretch # 294

1. Lie flat on your back on a bench, resting a dumbbell on your lower chest and grasping it with both hands.
2. Exhale, and raise the dumbbell off your chest.
3. Inhale, lock your arms straight, and lower the dumbbell over your head as close to the floor as possible.
4. Hold the stretch and relax.
5. Exhale, and return to the starting point.

ARMS

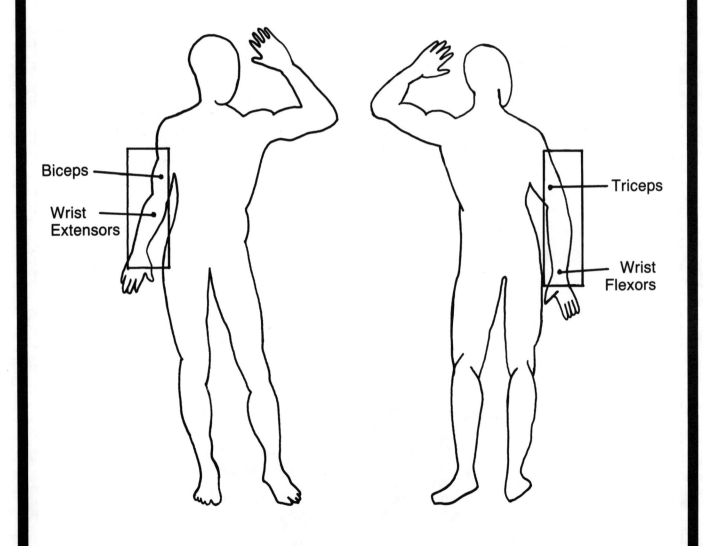

Biceps

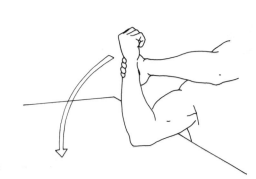

Stretch # 295

1. Sit upright, with one arm flexed 90 degrees and the elbow resting on a table.
2. Grasp your wrist with the opposite hand.
3. Exhale, and execute a maximal eccentric contraction of the biceps (contract the biceps as you stretch them with your other hand).
4. When your arm is fully extended, hold the stretch and relax.

Stretch # 296

1. Stand upright with your back to a doorframe.
2. Rest one hand against the doorframe with your arm externally rotated at the shoulder, your forearm extended, and your hand pronated with your thumb pointing down.
3. Exhale, and attempt to roll your biceps so they face upward.
4. Hold the stretch and relax.

Stretch # 297

1. Sit or stand by a table with your arm resting on the surface and your elbow flexed to 90 degrees while holding a light dumbbell.
2. Inhale, and slowly extend your elbow while contracting your biceps (eccentric contraction).
3. Hold the stretch and relax.
4. Exhale, and return the weight to the starting position.

■ This may result in muscle soreness!

Triceps

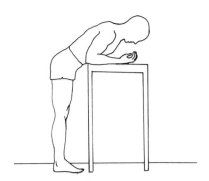

Stretch # 298

1. Stand upright with your forearms resting on a table.
2. Exhale, bend forward, and bring your shoulders to your wrists.
3. Hold the stretch and relax.

Stretch # 299

1. Sit or stand upright with one arm flexed and raised overhead next to your ear, and your hand resting on your shoulder blade.
2. Grasp your elbow with the opposite hand.
3. Exhale, and pull your elbow behind your head.
4. Hold the stretch and relax.

Stretch # 300

1. Sit or stand upright with one arm placed as far up on your back as possible.
2. Lift your other arm overhead while holding a folded blanket or towel, and flex your elbow.
3. Grasp the blanket or towel with your lower hand.
4. Inhale as you slowly pull your hands together.
5. Hold the stretch and relax.

Stretch # 301

1. Sit or stand upright with one arm placed as far up on your back as possible.
2. Lift your other arm overhead, flex your elbow, and interlock your fingers.
3. Hold the stretch and relax.

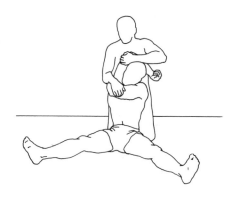

Stretch # 302

1. Sit upright on the floor with your legs straddled.
2. Raise your right arm, and flex it behind your head.
3. Flex your left arm across your chest.
4. Your partner kneels behind you with his or her hands grasping your elbows.
5. Inhale as your partner pulls down on your raised elbow and across on your opposite elbow. Communicate with your partner and use great care.
6. Hold the stretch and relax.

Stretch # 303

1. Sit or stand upright, with one arm flexed and raised overhead next to your ear, and your hand resting on your shoulder blade.
2. Your partner is positioned to your side with one hand grasping your wrist and the other holding your elbow.
3. Exhale as you allow your partner to raise your elbow and pull your wrist downward. Communicate with your partner and use great care.
4. Hold the stretch and relax.

Stretch # 304

1. Sit upright and hold a light dumbbell overhead with one hand as the opposite hand supports the elbow.
2. Inhale, and slowly lower the dumbbell behind your head.
3. Hold the stretch and relax.
4. Exhale, and return to the starting position.

Wrist Extensors (Brachioradialis)

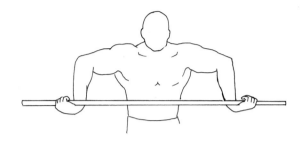

Stretch # 305

1. Kneel on the floor, flex your wrists, and place the tops of your hands on the floor.
2. Exhale, and lean against the floor.
3. Hold the stretch and relax.

Stretch # 306

1. Hold a pole above your head with your hands in an L-grip (the back of the hand faces up and the thumbs grasp under the pole).
2. Exhale and lower the pole to your waist while flexing your elbows.
3. Hold the stretch and relax.

Stretch # 307

1. Hang from a chin-up bar with your arms straight.
2. Release one hand at a time, and regrasp the bar in an L-grip (the back of the hand faces up and the thumb grasps under the bar).
3. Hold the stretch and relax.

Forearm Flexors

Stretch # 308

1. Sit or stand upright with your wrists flexed.
2. Place the heel of one hand against the upper portion of the fingers of your other hand.
3. Exhale, and press the heel of your hand against your fingers.
4. Hold the stretch and relax.

Stretch # 309

1. Kneel on the floor with your arms extended and fingers pointed away from your body.
2. Exhale, and lean backward.
3. Hold the stretch and relax.

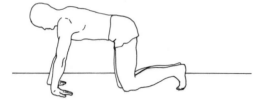

Stretch # 310

1. Kneel on the floor with your arms extended and your fingers pointed toward your body.
2. Exhale, and lean forward.
3. Hold the stretch and relax.

Stretch # 311

1. Kneel on the floor with your arms extended and the heel of each hand touching the other.
2. Exhale, and lean forward.
3. Hold the stretch and relax.

APPENDIX

Research (Harris, 1969) has proven that flexibility is specific and not a general body factor. That is, range of motion is specific to each joint in the body. So, for instance, an athlete may be flexible in the hips but tight in the shoulders, or tight in the right hip but flexible in the left hip.

Research (Iashvili, 1983) has verified that active flexibility has a higher correlation to the level of sports achievement ($r = 0.81$) than does passive mobility ($r = 0.69$).

Research (Iashvili, 1983) has verified that active flexibility values are lower than passive ones.

Research (Hardy, 1985; Iashvili, 1983; Tumanyan & Dzhanyan, 1984) has shown that the relationship between passive and active flexibility is dependent on the training methods.

Research (Bell & Hoshizaki, 1981) has found that females, especially children, tend to be more flexible than males.

Research (Bell & Hoshizaki, 1981; Sermeev, 1966) has shown that flexibility tends to decrease with age.

Research (Bell & Hoshizaki, 1981; Dummer, Vaccaro, & Clarke, 1985; Germain & Blair, 1983) has proven that senior adults benefit from flexibility training.

Research (Leighton, 1956; Massey & Chaudet, 1956; Wickstrom, 1963) has demonstrated that weight training does not decrease flexibility, and that in some instances it actually improves it.

Research (Alter, 1988; Clarke, 1975) reviews found that attempts to correlate flexibility to body proportions, body surface area, skinfold, and weight have yielded inconsistent results.

Research (Warren, Lehmann, & Koblanski, 1971 & 1976; LaBan, 1962) has found that elastic (recoverable) deformation is facilitated by high-force, short-duration stretching.

Research (Warren et al., 1971 & 1976; LaBan, 1962) has found that plastic (permanent) deformation is facilitated by low-force, long-duration stretching.

Research (LaBan, 1962; Rigby, 1964) has proven that as tissue temperature rises, stiffness decreases and extensibility increases.

Research (Akeson, Amiel, & Woo, 1980) has proven that immobilization results in the loss of extensibility and an increase in tissue stiffness.

Research (Moretz, Walters, & Smith, 1982) has failed to confirm the previous assumption that there is a correlation between laxity (looseness) test scores and knee injuries.

Akeson, W.H., Amiel, D., & Woo, S. (1980). Immobility effects on synovial joints: The pathomechanics of joint contracture. *Biorheology*, **17**(1/2), 95-110.

Alter, M.J. (1988). *Science of stretching*. Champaign, IL: Human Kinetics.

Bell, R.D., & Hoshizaki, T.B. (1981). Relationship of age and sex with range of motion of seventeen joint actions in humans. *Canadian Journal of Applied Sports Science*, **6**(4), 202-206.

Clarke, H. (1975). Joint and body range of movement. *Physical Fitness Research Digest*, **5**, 1-22.

Dummer, G.M., Vaccaro, P., & Clarke, D.H. (1985). Muscular strength and flexibility of two female master swimmers in the eighth decade of life. *The Journal of Orthopaedic and Sports Physical Therapy, **6***(4), 235-237.

Germain, N.W., & Blair, S.N. (1983). Variability of shoulder flexion with age, activity and sex. *The American Corrective Therapy Journal, **37***(6), 156-160.

Hardy, L. (1985). Improving active range of hip flexion. *Research Quarterly for Exercise and Sport, **56***(2), 111-114.

Harris, M.L. (1969). A factor analytic study of flexibility. *Research Quarterly, **40***(1), 62-70.

Iashvili, A.V. (1983). Active and passive flexibility in athletes specializing in different sports. *Soviet Sports Review, **18***(1), 30-32.

LaBan, M.M. (1962). Collagen tissue: Implications of its response to stress in vitro. *Archives of Physical Medicine and Rehabilitation, **43***(9), 461-465.

Leighton, J.R. (1956). Flexibility characteristics of males ten to eighteen years of age. *Archives of Physical and Mental Rehabilitation, **37***(8), 494-499.

Massey, B.A., & Chaudet, N.L. (1956). Effects of systematic, heavy resistance exercise on range of joint movement in young adults. *Research Quarterly, **28***(4), 352-356.

Moretz, A.J., Walters, R., & Smith, L. (1982). Flexibility as a predictor of knee injuries in college football players. *The Physician and Sportsmedicine, **10***(7), 93-97.

Rigby, B. (1964). The effect of mechanical extension under the thermal stability of collagen. *Biochimica et Biophysica Acta, **79***(SC 43008), 634-636.

Sermeev, B.V. (1966). Development of mobility in the hip joint in sportsmen. *Yessis Review, **2***(1), 16-17.

Tumanyan, G.S., & Dzhanyan, S.M. (1984). Strength exercises as a means of improving active flexibility of wrestlers. *Soviet Sports Review, **19***(3), 146-150.

Warren, C.G., Lehmann, J.F., & Koblanski, J.N. (1971). Elongation of rat tail tendon: Effect of load and temperature. *Archives of Physical Medicine and Rehabilitation, **52***(3), 465-474.

Warren, C.G., Lehmann, J.F., & Koblanski, J.N. (1976). Heat stretch procedures: An evaluation using rat tail tendon. *Archives of Physical Medicine and Rehabilitation, **57***(3), 122-126.

Wickstrom, R.L. (1963). Weight training and flexibility. *Journal of Health, Physical Education and Recreation, **34***(2), 61-62.

ABOUT THE AUTHOR

A former gymnast, coach, and nationally certified men's gymnastics judge, Michael J. Alter is an expert on the subject of stretching. His previous book, *Science of Stretching*, continues to receive rave reviews from athletes, coaches, trainers, and physical therapists. In *Sport Stretch*, Alter expands on his earlier work by mapping out an easy-to-follow, sport-specific stretching plan every healthy athlete can use to improve performance and prevent injury.

Michael Alter earned his MS in health education from Florida International University in 1976. He has taught physical education and coached gymnastics for several years in Florida; at present, he teaches high school in Miami. In his leisure time, Michael enjoys listening to classical music, bicycling, working out with weights, and studying sports medicine.